HUMANS
AND
FACTS

HUMANS
AND
FACTS

2nd Edition

Mehdi Alem, M.Sc., Ph.D.

Humans and Facts

Printed in the United States of America
ISBN 979-8-89633-110-0 (paperback)
ISBN 979-8-89633-111-7 (ebook)

This is a work of fiction. Unless otherwise indicated, all the names, characters, businesses, places, events and incidents in this book are either the product of the author's imagination and are purely coincidental.

Because of the dynamic nature of the Internet, any web addresses or links contained in this book may have changed since publication and may no longer be valid. The views expressed in this work are solely those of the author and do not necessarily reflect the views of the publisher, and the publisher hereby disclaims any responsibility for them.

2026.01.05

Page Solutions
124 Rock Crystal Ln,
Lakeside Park,
KY 41017A
United States

PAGE
SOLUTIONS

Table of Contents

This book is dedicated to:

*My family and
people who believe in humanity.*

Knowledge is the key for success.

CHAPTER ONE

Introduction

Today is Sept. 19, 2001. It was only 8 days ago when several hijacked planes crashed into the World Trade Center and the Pentagon, killing over 3,000 innocent people. I have followed news related to this event immediately after its onset. In fact, except for the time, which I slept, I am listening, watching and reading the news on the radio, TV, or internet. Different versions of one subject are discussed several times per day. Every individual in the United States and maybe in the whole world are talking about this subject. I think it is normal to talk about such a new, horrible, and incredible subject. A small number of people are happy and of course most of the whole world population is sad. The subject is very hot and each person analyzes the whole story based on his/her knowledge. I personally think the subject is hotter than what people think. A small number of individuals in their own world reached a conclusion and decide to kill themselves and thousands of ordinary people. We may think that the victims were ordinary people. To those who initiated such a mess, the victims were not ordinary individuals. They tried to kill the maximum number of men and women in the shortest possible time. It seems their targets have been individuals who were in the business of finance and military. What does this mean? Was their act related to money or arms? Each ten minutes the radio emphasizes that the individual responsible for this action were terrorists and they were from Arab countries. Also, each ten minutes we are getting the news about stock market and how fast it is going down. It was only two days ago when everybody in the United States was talking about how to keep the market unchanged and fighting with terrorists by holding the stocks. It seems people talk but do not act. If the economy is in a trouble why should people keep their stocks? What does this mean? Is the economy the first target and subject? The news media each five minutes announce that the terrorists were Moslem and were supported by specific countries. Nobody even mentioned that the population of these countries are themselves under pressure by their own governments. Nobody talks about the terrorists' intentions and reasons for their acts. News also indicates that in retaliation to a terrorist' act, a significant number of businesses whose owners were from certain religions or races was attached. There were cases that individuals were killed by mistake because the killers judged the race or the religion of the victims only based on the color of skin, having beard or certain appearances. It is unbelievable. People kill each other solely based on their own judgment. Is this type of behavior acceptable? If killing over 3000 men and women is considered a terrorist action, what term is used if only an individual is killed by mistake?

If we deeply analysis what is going on, we will see that human kills human, no matter if one person is killed or thousands. Think for a moment. Do not you see a similarity between human behaviors with those of animals? I do not see any similarity. Animals rarely kill or destroy their own species. Animals use their power only to find food and survive. In fact, the easiest definition of animals is "animals are

2

always resting except when they are searching for food". Of course, the meaning of the food for animal is really something to eat and live. We, humans consider ourselves the most civilized type of life on the surface of the earth and therefore put ourselves in a position to do whatever we want. We are not even acting like animals. In addition to food, we need thousands of other items. We need a place to live in, we need lands for agriculture, we need gas to put in our cars, and so on. Simply, we need thousands of various items. To reach to our goals, we divide ourselves into various races and different religions and try to hold certain territories. It is obvious that only those groups who have better lands, more knowledge, advanced social background etc., have easier access to what they want. Territory and belief in different religions are additional factors. At birth, we do not belong to any specific religion and do not even know where in the whole universe we are. Someone decides who we are and plan for our future. During childhood, our parents transfer their beliefs to us. Our genetic information programs our biological functions but we are highly affected by surrounding environment. Our societies have direct influence on our behaviors and personalities.

I am originally trained as a biologist therefore, as far as I remember; I have always been interested in the life on the earth and especially out in the universe. I have been mainly interested in advanced forms of life or intelligent life. Since the most advanced level of life on the earth is humans, from my childhood I have been thinking about the origin and behaviors of humans. During my life, I have seen different places, individuals, and cultures and overall thought extensively about life as we know and life beyond our planet. Obviously, I also thought why out of over 2,000,000 different species living on the earth only humans (*Homo sapiens*) are considered the most advanced one.

We humans follow certain rules, live in certain regions, and have different religions. What about other species? Do they have their own religions? If not, what makes them so different? Is God only associated with human beings? Do other species have the same God? Do they know where they are in the universe? Do other species know anything about God? Does God exist? If God does exist, what is it? Does he really control us? Does he know what we are doing? Does he care what we do? If we do something wrong, will we be punished by him? If there is "a" God, why do different humans on the earth have different meanings for him? Some people think their God is made of stone (statue), a group of them think their God is another human, still there are individuals who think their God is made of nothing and is at the same time everywhere. Which one of these groups is right? Who gave permission to humans to destroy other forms of life at any rates, which they want to satisfy their needs?

These questions and thousands of similar ones have always been in my mind. During my childhood and later while I was in school; I was thinking about these questions most of the time but did not have sufficient knowledge to answer my own questions. Gradually, and in the course of my education, I expanded my knowledge. Needless to mention that increase in my knowledge had reverse effect on me and created more questions for me. Of course, like thousands of people, I could say this is life. My parents brought me to this world and one day I will die. Life is too short to worry about it. I did not choose this approach. To find the answers to my questions, I tried to read subjects about the universe, solar system, physical and chemical structure of the universe and our planet, life on our planet, origin of life on earth, evolution of life, human beings, evolution of mankind, our behaviors, our religions, birth, death, after death, end of life on earth, and finally end of the universe.

These questions and partial answers to them led me to a point that I decided to somehow express my ideas about life on Earth. I knew that during the history of mankind, in many occasions, there were individuals who brought up important subjects but nobody cared about their ideas at the time. I also knew that sometimes these ideas were accepted many years later.

The first thing which is interesting for me is a fact that humans have been at war with each other at any given time for thousands of years. The fights between early humans were mostly for food, territory, and finding mates. Early humans used stone tools and later different types of tools to fight with each other. These days, in addition to hundreds of different types of tools, religions are also used as tools in wars! If we review the history of humans, we will soon realize that real improvement in our knowledge has been only during the last 300 years and mainly the last 50 years. This period is nothing compared with the age of life on earth. Interestingly, during the last 50 years along with improvement in technology, the relations between different populations and various religions got worse. Only in the last 50 years humans faced at least 20 major wars. I think we should ask ourselves why this is the case? Will it be possible to reach to a stable peace and use our efforts to improve humanity? Is it possible to eliminate any types of fight? Is it possible to control religions? Is it possible to make a united world and destroy all borders? If we deeply study the behavior of humans, we will see that soon they not only destroy themselves but gradually will make drastic changes in the lives of other organisms on the earth too. I think we can make useful changes if we accurately study the roots of problems and especially understand human behaviors, needs, and relations. It is obvious that our study should be based on facts and especially scientific data. To reach to our goals, we should know our species; find out who we are, why we are on the earth, and our future. In this book I tried to scientifically analyze the presence of humans on the earth and their relations. My primary goal is to analyze "humans" and hopefully reach a conclusion for a better future for mankind.

I had the idea of writing this book for several years but I could not do it because of many reasons. First, I realized that it was not so easy to write what I exactly thought. Writing about subjects related to science is much easier than writing about our ordinary life. Second, can I write about religions, races, God and these types of sensitive subjects? In societies where the subject of human evolution is still under question, how can one talk about other more sensitive subjects such as the wrong influences of several religious leaders on the ordinary people? The ability to accept one's death is easier for those who expect a rewarding afterlife. Can we really ask what is after life? All these questions and subjects were always preventing me to transfer what I thought onto the pages of a book. In the societies where even writing a specific type of fiction is prohibited how dare a person to write something, which may not be a fiction. Third, and the worst part, what about if I write something that religious people and politicians do not like? Of course, all these issues were several times more problematic while I was in my own native country. After I immigrated to the United States, I found this country relatively a free society; therefore, sometimes in 1994 I started to write notes about the relations between humans and the future of life on the earth. Of course, I could not complete my notes due to engagement with my own work.

On Sept. 11, 2001 while I watched the tragedy in the World Trade Center, I could not believe my own eyes. How come several individuals who had talents to be pilots decided to use their talents and kill themselves along with others? Why in American society where there are thousands of highly educated scholars no one deeply search for the reasons? Why did the same people who hate terrorist actions, do the same action in a smaller scale. We know that the United States, with its relatively short history, contributed more than any nations in the world in the improvement of science and technology. In this country, people work very hard and are highly productive but still they are the main target. American people ask themselves, why are we hated so much? Something must be wrong. It seems the world and mankind really entered a new phase of relations.

I think before judging about these problems we should first find the reasons. We should scientifically study human behaviors, history of mankind and our relations. Humans have a dark future in front of them and our species is the most problematic form of life on the earth. I also think, most of recent issues, which we are facing now, are related to the nature of our species. We cannot easily find solutions for the problems and correct issues related to our natural behavior. We should study different cultures and search for reasons. After we find the reasons, we should try to correct them. We should not be afraid to accept that human beings, our species, are really an advanced and sophisticated animal and therefore should follow the rules of the animal kingdom. It may be hard to accept that human beings act worse than animals. It may be extremely hard to accept that religions, true or false, are transferred from our parents to us, as a heredity factor. We should accept that these days' religions are used as a tool by different cultures to reach their goals. It may be unbelievable for a group of people if someone proves that after our death time stops for us. We never come back and never go anywhere else. It may be hard to accept that even the atoms, which build our bodies, do not belong to us anymore after we die. The soul is not real, and even if there is something after death, its nature is not clear for us. Most of ideas transferred to us by our grand— grandparents do not have any scientific support or simply any real meaning. Why do we still follow them and believe them. Why do we believe those ideas, which began several thousand years ago? Why are there leaders, who order killing thousands of innocent people only because they have different religion, race or do not believe what the leaders want? Even more problematic, why are there individuals who are ready to kill themselves and thousands of other people for a reward such as directly going to heaven? What is heaven and where is it? Does it exist?

Is not it better if we try to find answers to these "WHY". Is not it better to believe what is close to reality? Even if we want to stay in our own unrealistic world, is it necessary to emphasize on our ideas and by force try to change other people's ideas? There may be highly educated people who disagree with me. I may be criticized by individuals who think people on the surface of the earth understand what is going on around them and therefore we should leave them to stay in their own world and let them believe what they want. In fact this is the most disturbing thing, which should be seriously considered. The people who do not know the facts about life are the main tools, which are used by religious and/or countries' leaders for promotion of certain belief and planning certain actions. We should try to educate people. It is true that we cannot send every individual to universities and force them to learn all subjects for themselves. What we can do is to educate the right things and prevent wrong doing. I am indeed happy to have relative freedom in the United States to write these words.

In the following pages I will try to briefly write some notes about several subjects associated with humans. I hope the readers find these notes useful. To reach to my goal, I need to briefly discuss several basic scientific topics. The topics will be, the universe and its origin, existence of other universe(s)!, creator of our universe, our solar system and its physical and chemical properties, earth and its specifications, matter and energy, life and its origin, varieties in life, relation between matter and life, human beings and their relation to animals, earth before our existence and after our death, relation between time and our existence, biology of human beings, effect of environment on us, mind and belief, ecology and our environment, our relation with the environment, life out of the solar system, travel to other solar systems, UFO, after death experience, effect of religions on human beings, our behaviors and similarity between human and animals, human evolution, distribution of human beings on the earth, border and countries, races and colors, needs for food, war and peace, overall history of mankind, improvement in life style, future of human beings on earth, increase in population and its consequences, and finally suggestions for corrections. It is obvious that for covering all mentioned subjects, much knowledge and skills are needed. Therefore, I tried to explain each section in the simplest possible words. There are thousands of individuals whose knowledge about each one of the above topics are much more than mine. I hope these individuals forgive me for simplicity in writing.

CHAPTER TWO

Universe: Its Origin and Future

What is the universe? The simplest definition for universe is a place, which we are in it. This place consists of billions of stars, planets, moons, black holes, particles, different radiations, and energy. We can say: Universe is "existance". It is not exactly known if this universe has a limit or, in other words, has a border! We do not know the exact history of our universe. We also do not know if our universe is the only one. There may be other "universes" right after our universe. Our technology currently does not allow us to even think about it. In the following pages I will review the latest scientific information regarding the structure of our universe and its limit. There may be other "universes" with completely different structures. Who knows? With our existing knowledge we hardly understand the fourth dimension (time). How can we find the details of such a complicated subject? There may be places even in our own universe, which are associated with dimensions "n".

The first question, which one may ask, is: how and by whom our universe was made? The answer to this question is not easy. In one sentence we may say—nobody knows and I think nobody will ever know; however, if we do not know or understand the answer to our questions, we should not simply say "God created the universe". At least we should ask ourselves why he did it. What were his intentions? Is the existence of our universe a mistake in an experiment taken place in a laboratory in another universe? Was the God performing an experiment when universe was created? Is the outcome what he wanted? Were his works successful and exactly the way, which he planned? How could he plan such a huge experiment? What was the goal for his work? How did he obtain such power? Who is he? If he is actually in another universe or "world", how was that universe or "world" created and by whom? What is he made of? Does he care about what he did? Is he still interested in his work? Nearly in all advanced religions God is referred to as a kind and highly powerful "something". How did we reach this conclusion? Did he himself transfer his ideas to us? Finally, if God created our universe and had enough time to plan and design all details in one planet (earth) out of billions and billions of other planets, who created him? So, it is not easy to simply say: God did it. If we do not know the answers to the above questions, what shall we do? Logic tells us we should find the answers or try to at least find the best possible answers using more reliable methods. We should not simply agree with ideas, which do not have any basic supports. The easiest questions, which we should ask ourselves are: Are we alone in the universe? If there are other types of life in the universe, are they like us? Do they follow the same rules as we do? Does God have specific rules for each section of the universe? Even if there are other sorts of life in our universe, how many planets harbor life? What is the use of other planets, which do not have life of any sort? Have we ever asked ourselves this question: If we take a hypothetical straight line and continue forever where would we go? Is there any limit or end for the universe(s)? If the answer is yes, is there any border there? If there is a border what is after that border?

I think there are thousands of unanswered questions like those mentioned above. So, what shall we do? Did we come to this world to live for an average of about 50 years and follow several baseless rules and then die? Or we should think and use our brain to expand our knowledge and at least find the answers to several of our simple questions? Logic is in the favor of the second approach.

Whenever we want to solve a problem, we should first investigate the problem. Can we solve our problem by doing experiment(s) and then analyze the data? Yes, in certain cases we can. For example, we can perform an experiment and prove the force of gravity but we cannot perform an experiment and create a universe. Of course, there are problems, which are neither so easy nor so hard. We can use our knowledge to predict the events or use a hypothesis to explain problems. Example, we really do not know the exact time and method by which our universe was created. Neither should we simply say someone did it. Experts may be able to help us; however, even experts do not have the right answers to many of our questions. They may be able to present believable or doable ideas. So, keep in your mind, first learn, and then accept. Do not believe subjects which do not have logical supports. In the following pages, I do not emphasize on ideas, which do not have any acceptable or meaningful supports.

It is believed that about 14 billion years ago the space an time came into existence and with its existence the time started. In 1965 two astronomers at Bell laboratory in Holmdel, NJ presented a theory named, "Big Bang", to explain how the cosmos begins. The discovery of the Big Bang was somehow an accident and was based on a cosmic microwave background radiation. Based on the Big Bang theory, the universe started from an initial "Big Bang" and gave birth to time, space, energy and matter as they exist in the universe now. The bursts or explosive period took a period of time around 10^{-40} second (0.0000000000000000000000000000000000000001 second) and initiated from an inflation of matter smaller than an atom with no charge to matter as big as an orange. During such an extremely short period of time (around 10^{-30} second), the whole matter and energy as we now know was formed by a subsequent expansion of the same orange –sized matter. At a time, close to 10^{-10} second a part of energy formed up to this stage was in the form of electromagnetic radiations—radio waves, visible light, ultraviolet rays and x-ray. Quarks, which are sub—atomic matters produced protons (positive charge) and neutron (no charge) and a combination of protons and neutrons later ended making nuclei of all atoms. Each atom consists of a certain number of protons, and several neutrons, which is usually close to, the number of protons and several much smaller-size matters with negative charge called electrons. In a neutralized form of any atom, the number of electrons is equal to the number of protons. An ion is an atom, which lost electron. An atom, which lost an electron, is an ion with a positive charge and of course electron is an ion with a negative charge. The materials which exist in the present universe, including what is used in our bodies was made in an extremely small fraction of a second about 15-20 million years ago. The simplest atoms such as hydrogen, (one proton and one electron), deuterium (an isotope of hydrogen with one proton, one neutron and one electron), and helium (two protons, two neutrons, and two electrons) were made in a time around 1 second. This huge size matter and energy was then gradually packed to form the first generation of stars during the first 1 billion years after the Big Bang (about 30,000,000,000,000,000 seconds) and in about 10 billion years galaxies were shaped. It is believed that our sun which is a star among over 200 billion stars in the Milky Way (our galaxy) was formed about 5 billion years ago. Our solar system which consists of sun (in the center) and nine planets around it was formed around 4.6 million years ago in a distance equal to 30,000 light-years (about 3×10^{17} kilometers) from the center of the Milky Way.

Our solar system was made from dust and gas, which were first in the form of clouds. By the force of its own gravity, the clouds contracted and subsequent rotation and the action of gravity in the center caused formation of concentrated material. Gradually, the center reached to a high pressure and a temperature of 6 million Celsius finally producing sun. The rest of clouds gradually and in a slow process aggregated and formed relatively small-size planets around the sun. It is believed that a mars-size planet collided with earth and caused the birth of the moon. The condensation of gases far from the sun caused formation of giant planets such as Jupiter and Saturn. A relatively small portion of clouds produced smaller pieces—asteroids—mainly between Mars and Jupiter.

The planets around the sun in the order of their distances to the sun are Mercury, Venus, Earth, Mars, Jupiter, Saturn, Uranus, Neptune, and Pluto. Of these plants, Jupiter is the biggest and Pluto is the smallest one. Also, except Mercury and Venus, the rest of the planets have at least one moon. It is obvious that the closest planet to the sun (Mercury) is the hottest and Pluto is the coldest planet. The sun, which is a star, along with its nine planets, formed our solar system, which is in the far end of the Milky Way. The sun mainly consists of light atoms. The energy produced in the sun is the result of fusion reaction of these light atoms. It is believed that in a chain reaction starting with proton- proton (the nucleus of a hydrogen atom contains 1 proton) interaction, deuterium, which is another isotope of hydrogen consisting of one proton and one neutron, is formed. The deuterium is then combined with another proton and produces a nucleus of helium-3 (the nucleus of helium-3 consists of two protons and one neutron). Finally, two helium-3 reacts with each other and produce one helium-4 (the nucleus of helium-4 consists of two protons and two neutrons) and two protons which are available to initiate the same cycle of reactions. As the results of these chain reactions, other particles such as neutrinos (an elementary particle with no charge and relatively low mass) and positron (a particle with the size of electron with a positive charge— anti-electron) are produced. The main product of the proton-proton reaction in the sun is the release of high-energy gamma rays. This reaction, which is similar to what, we know as hydrogen bomb occurs at a temperature of 6-million-degree C. In the core of the sun the temperature is around 14-million-degree C and therefore it is a suitable environment for proton-proton reaction. The gamma rays produced in the core travel slowly toward the surface of the sun and because of their interaction with particles weaken and change to X-ray, ultraviolet, visible light, and infrared light. Most of the observable energy on the surface of the sun is visible light. The radiation produced by the sun, travel to all directions and obviously reach the earth. Earth receives visible light which is needed for photosynthesis, infrared light which produces heat and ultraviolet light which has the property to cause certain changes in the chemical reactions. We will later discuss in more details the effects of these lights on the life on earth.

Not all stars are like our sun and not all suns necessarily have planets. The nearest sun—like stars to our solar system are Proxima Centauri, Alpha Centauri A, Epsilon Eridani, and Tau Ceti which are respectively, 4.0 ,4.4, 10.8, and 11.8 light years far from us. Later we will discuss in more details the possibility of life around these stars and the chance of contact with them.

A group of about 200 billion stars, billions of unknown planets, comets, moons, star clusters and nebulas form a galaxy. All stars, which we can see in the sky on a clear night, are parts of our Milky Way Galaxy. It is obvious that we only see objects, where their lights reach us. There are billions and billions of particles which are not visible to us. There are also unknown numbers of black holes (celestial objects of extremely intense gravity) in our galaxy. Of these objects, the most interesting ones are the planets, places that may harbor life. Unfortunately, because of relatively small size, darkness, and extreme distance to us, we cannot see these planets. Recent improvements in astronomy confirmed the existence of planets in other solar systems. It is believed that at least 200 billion galaxies made our universe. This means that there are at least 4×10^{22} stars (4 0,000,000,000,000,000,000,000) in our universe and if in average each star has only one planet, there should be the same numbers of planets in our universe and earth is one of them. Doing a simple math calculation considering the probability, we will conclude that a significant number of these planets may have some sort of life. We will get back to this subject in the following pages. The Milky Way Galaxy has a disc shape with a diameter of about 100,000 and thickness of 10,000 light years. Its mass is about one trillion 750 billion solar masses. There are billions of galaxies larger than our galaxy and billions, which are smaller. The nearest large galaxy to us is 2.9 million light years away. Our galaxy is a part of a group of galaxies named local group. Simply, billions of galaxies distributed in a huge expanding spherical space with a diameter of 15-20 billion light years (about $189,216,000,000,000,000,000,000 = 1.9 \times 10^{23}$ kilometers) and this is named universe. Every part of the universe is in move. Later we will discuss in more details about the distances between stars and galaxies and explore the possibility of traveling between planets in search of extra-terrestrial life.

Now, we go back to the history and future of the universe. By passing time gradually stars, including our own sun die. Our sun is the largest object in our solar system and contains more than 99.8% of the total mass of our solar system. At present, the sun consists of about 75% hydrogen, 25% helium, and 0.1everything else by mass. As far as we now know hydrogen gradually converts to helium and produces the energy. Each second the energy output by sun is 386 billion billion megawatts which means each second 700,000,000 tons of hydrogen convert to 695,000,000 tons of helium and 5,000,000 tons energy in the form of gamma rays are released. In addition to heat and light, the sun also emits a low-density stream of charged particles (mostly electrons and protons). These particles and other cosmic rays can have dramatic effects on the earth. One of the effects is change in the genetic structure of living organisms. This subject will be discussed in more detail later. The sun is about 4.5—5 billion years old. Since its birth it has used up about half of the hydrogen in its core. This means that it will continue to be what it is for another 5 billion years. During this period its luminosity will approximately double and get bigger. The sun eventually will run out of hydrogen fuel and will be forced into changes, which, finally result in the destruction of the earth (probably the creation of a new nebula). Some stars die a violent death when they explode. Such an explosion is called supernova and it is during such a process that relatively heavy elements form by fusion from smaller atoms. Our solar system is a second or third generation of stars born from the fallout of defunct stars. This means that materials used in our bodies might have been used in other bodies in another solar system, which existed billions of years ago.

In about 10^{30} years after the Big Bang, planets detach from stars and planets and stars escaped from galaxies. Gradually, most of matter in the universe change to neutron stars and black holes. In about 10^{40} years the protons decay and eventually in about 10^{50} years after the Big Bang, only black holes remain which finally evaporate into radiations. In about 10^{100} years (one with a hundred zeros on its right side!) the dark era starts. Currently only particles such as electrons, positrons, neutrons, and radiations are scattered in a very vast area. At this time electrons (negative charge) and positrons (positive charge, anti- electron) may forms atoms, which are bigger than our universe as it is today? The universe at this stage is dark and cold. Who knows what will happen after this period? Maybe a new and completely different universe will be born.

In summary, the universe is made of billions of galaxies and each galaxy is made of billions of stars. In the universe, there are also different types of energy mostly in the form of radiations. The universe was born in an extremely small fraction of a second (10^{-40} sec) and will "die" in about 10^{100} years. Several stars in the galaxies formed solar systems. Solar systems and galaxies are very far away from each other. In our solar system nine planets are orbiting the sun. As far as we know, at present time, only earth harbors life. We do not know why and by whom the universe was born. Equally, we do not know if other "universes" exist. The actual boundary for our universe is not established.

Recent studies suggest a new theory in the subject of theoretical physics which is named "string theory". This theory, which is now one of the hottest subjects in modern physics—was presented during the last thirty to forty years. This theory basically says that everything in the whole universe as we know consists of strings. Strings that are extremity small are like strings. We will never be able to see a string at all, and its presence can only be proven by theoretical formula.

"To give you an idea about how small a string is, if we imagine that a man is 2 meters tall, a string is 0.00000000000000000000000 000000000001 meter or 10^{-35} meter.

"It may help to say that the whole universe is 10^{27} meters, which is 1,000,000,000,000,000,000,000,000,000 meters.

"Another example: If we hypothetically imagine the size of a proton as big as our solar system, in size comparison, a string will be as big as the size of a bicycle!

It is estimated that our universe consists of about 10×10^{90} particles, which means only in our universe. The string theory also describes the presence of 10^{500} separate universes (multiverses or parallel universes) , with different constants of nature and even different laws of physics. Many physicists think this is a weakness of the string theory, but *scientists* think it could help us understand why our universe is so well suited to life.

In the last thirty to forty years, our knowledge about astrophysics and theoretical physics has been exponentially increasing. Now, in addition to string theory new subjects such as M-theory, parallel universes, and quantum physics as discussed. Parallel universes theory states that a significant number of these universes are exactly like our universe. It also states that a number of these universes share space with us. The parallel universes theory which is also known as "multiverse" states that many universes exist parallel to each other.

Recent observations of the three—dimensional galaxy distribution and the microwave background studies have shown that the arrangement of matter gives way to dull uniformity on large scales. The most distant visible objects in our universe are now about 4 x 10^{26} meters away. The entire universe which we call it our own universe is 10^{27} meters. This means that other universes should be away from 10^{27} meters. This assumption underlies the estimate that our closest identical copy universe is at least 10 x 10^{28} meters away. It is also assumed that about 10^{92} meters away, there should be a sphere and in about 10^{118} meters away there should be an entire 'volume' identical to ours.

Generally, scientists have discussed and divided parallel universes into as many as four distinct types or levels:

Level 1 parallel universes: The idea of level 1 parallel universes basically says that space is so big that the rules of probability imply that surely, somewhere else out there, are other planets exactly like Earth. In fact, an infinite universe would have infinitely many planets, which on some of them, the events that play out would be virtually identical to those on our own Earth. We do not see these other universes because our cosmic vision is limited by the speed of light—the ultimate speed limit. Light started traveling now of the big bang, about 14 billion years ago, and so we cannot see any further than about 14 billion light-years.

In other words, level 1 parallel universes do exist, but reaching one is virtually impossible. For one thing, we would not know where to look for one because, by definition, level 1 parallel universes are so far away that no message can ever get from us to them, or them to us. Observers living in the level I parallel universes experience the same laws of physics as we do, but with different initial conditions. The level 1parallel universes are essentially infinitely big and contains matter at roughly the same distribution as we see it throughout our own universe. Considering an infinite amount of space, it stands the reason that there exists more universe in which an exact duplicate of our world—and, in fact, our entire visible universe—exists.

Level 2 parallel universes: In a level 2 parallel universes, regions of space are continuing to undergo an inflation phase. Because of the continuing inflationary phase in these universes, space between us and the other universes is literally expanding faster than the speed of light—and they are, therefore, completely unreachable.

Theories which present reasons to believe that level 2 parallel universes may exist recall that the quantum fluctuations in the early universe's vacuum energy caused bubble universes to be created all over the place, expanding through their inflation stages at different rates. Based on this theory, findings of eternal inflation mean that when inflation starts, it produces not just one universe, but an infinite number of universes.

Generally, level 2 parallel universes or inflation bubbles describes separate universes spring up as bubbles of space time undergoing its own form of expansion, under the rules dictated by inflation theory. The laws of physics in these universes could be very different from our own. These infinite universes are sometimes called bubble universes even though they are irregular-shaped, and not round.

Level 3 parallel universes: A Level 3 parallel universe is a consequence of the many world's interpretation. Level 3 parallel universes are different from the level 1 and level 2 because they take place in the same space and time as our own universe, but you still have no way to access them. We assume, we have never had and will never have contact with any level 1 or level 2 universe, but we are continually in contact with level 3. According to what level 3 parallel universes states, these separate, coexisting universes interfere with each other, yielding the bizarre quantum behaviors.

Level 4 parallel universes: A level 4 parallel universe is the strangest place of all, because it would follow fundamentally different mathematical laws of nature than our universe. In short, any universe that physicists can get to work out on paper would exist in level 4, based on the mathematical democracy principle: Any universe that is mathematically possible has equal possibility of existing.

Generally, the level 4 parallel universes are ones which are governed by different equations from those that govern our universe. In other words, level 4 contains truly weird parallel universes, ones which differ from the others by having fundamentally different laws of physics.

The scientific theories of the parallel universes, therefore, form a four-level hierarchy, in which universes become progressively more different from ours. They might have different initial conditions (Level 1); different physical constants and particles (Level 2); or different physical laws (Level 4). It is ironic that level 3 is the one that has drawn the most fire in the past decades, because it is the only one that adds no qualitatively new types of universes.

CHAPTER THREE

Earth and Life on Earth

In the sixteenth century it was discovered that earth is a planet. Earth is the third planet from the sun. It is the fifth largest planet in our solar system with a mass of 5.98 x 10^{24} kilograms. Earth is divided into several layers with distinct chemical and seismic properties. Two main layers of the earth are the mantle and the core. The part that we inhabit is a tiny fraction of the whole earth. The earth is composed of various proportions of 103 different types of atoms. A small number of these atoms (heavy ones) are man- made and do not naturally exist. The core is probably composed mostly of iron and the upper mantle is mainly calcium and aluminum. Earth is the densest planet in the solar system and its surface is very young. In a relatively short period of the last 500,000,000 years, erosion and tectonic processes destroyed and recreated most of the existing earth's surface and thereby eliminated almost all traces of earlier geologic surface history. The oldest fossils of living organisms found on the earth are less than 3.9 billion years old. There is no documented record of the critical period when life was first getting started on the earth. The earth is about 150 million kilometers away from the sun and light from the sun takes about 8 minutes to reach to the earth (light travel 300,000 kilometer/ sec., or 9.46 trillion kilometers in one year). The diameter of earth is about 12756 kilometers and it has a rotation of 23.9345 hours around itself. The orbital period of earth is 365.256 days. The earth has one moon.

Seventy-one per cent of earth's surface is covered by water and 97% of that is salty oceans. Only a small portion of the earth's water is fresh water. This includes such things as rivers, lakes, and groundwater. Water consists of hydrogen and oxygen. Earth is the only planet on which water can exist in liquid form, though there may be liquid water beneath the surface of Europa (one of Jupiter's moons) too. Of course, liquid water is essential for life on the earth, as we know it.

Around the earth up to about 100 kilometers is called atmosphere. Atmosphere consists of several gases mainly, 78% nitrogen, 21% oxygen, 1% argon and about 0.03% carbon dioxide. There was probably a very much larger amount of carbon dioxide in the earth's atmosphere when the earth was first formed, but it has since been almost all incorporated into carbonate rocks and to a lesser extent dissolved into the oceans and consumed by living plants. Biological processes now maintain the balance of carbon dioxide in the atmosphere. The tiny amount of carbon dioxide resident in the atmosphere at any time is extremely important to the maintenance of the earth's surface temperature via the greenhouse effect. The greenhouse effect raises the average surface temperature about 35 degrees C above what it would otherwise be. Without the greenhouse affect the oceans would freeze and life as we know would be impossible. The presence of free oxygen is quite remarkable from a chemical point of view. Oxygen is a very reactive gas and under "normal" circumstances would quickly combine with other elements. The oxygen in the earth's atmosphere is produced and maintained by biological processes. Without life there would be no free oxygen. The earth has a modest magnetic field produced by electric currents in the outer core. The earth's magnetic field and its interaction with the solar wind produce the Van Allen radiation belts, a pair of doughnut shaped rings of ionized gas trapped in the orbit around the earth.

If we look at the earth's specifications, we will soon understand why our planet could support life and other planets in our solar system could not (Maybe, in the past Mars did). On the earth, the temperature is not too high or too low. Earth contains lots of water and water can be present at the same time in three forms of solid, liquid and gas. For an active life, as we know it, water should be in the form of liquid, something which is abundant on the earth. However, ¾ of earth surface is covered by water, still there are places on the earth, which are solid and can support terrestrial life. Imagine if the earth was 100% covered by water. In this case we might still have thousands of different species in the oceans, but no intelligent life the way that we know it could form. Atmosphere consists of nitrogen, oxygen, and carbon dioxide. All these gases are needed for existence of life on the earth. The formation of life on the earth will be discussed in more detail later.

It is obvious that the most interesting and fascinating part of the earth is life on earth. What is life? We do not have a simple definition for life. We may simply say if a combination of certain numbers of different atoms, as a package, is able to follow certain rules, have special specifications, and show specific functions, that package is alive. The main characteristics of a living organism are: (1) the ability to use simple or complicated chemicals components (generally named food) and convert them to the chemicals, which are needed to make the body. (2) The ability to directly or indirectly obtain energy from surrounding environment and use it for synthesis of certain chemicals in the body and for daily functions. (3) The ability of reproduction or producing new living organism(s). (4) The ability of having some sort of movements. (5) The ability to grow and increase the size. To obtain food, living organisms should have some sort of movement, which may involve fighting with other organisms. The above factors are signs of life. This means that any matter, which does not show these functions, is not considered alive. Later we will see that in spite of their weaknesses to independently perform the above functions, viruses are considered living organisms. Life is in fact a cumulative product of interactions and relations among different kinds of chemicals. These chemicals are made of atoms and all atoms used in life are originated from the earth. These atoms (elements) in the forms of simple or complicated chemical components are used by living organisms. Out of 92 different natural elements on the earth 25 of them are essential for life. Of these 25, four of them are making nearly 96% of living matter. These four elements are carbon, hydrogen, oxygen, and nitrogen. Phosphorus, sulfur, calcium, potassium, sodium, chlorine and magnesium are other elements the account for the remaining 3.99% of living organisms. The rest, which is 0.01% of the total weight, consists of other elements including, iodine, iron, boron, chromium, cobalt, copper, fluorine, magnesium, and zinc, which collectively are referred to as trace elements. Of these elements, carbon is considered the basic element of life on the earth. This means that all major components needed for life on the earth contain carbon. We should keep in mind that life in other planets (if it exists) may not necessarily be carbon—dependent. Living organisms mainly in the forms of chemical compounds absorbs these elements. In the bodies of living organisms these elements should react with each other by certain organized pathways. This means that a mixture of above elements in an unorganized form is not a living matter. In fact, after our death, all elements used in our bodies are the same as when we were alive. The only major difference is the fact that a number of main reactions, which usually take place (out of millions), stop their normal pathways after death.

The main components of our bodies, which make over 99.90% of total mass, are water, proteins, nucleic acids, lipids, and sugars. Of these components proteins and nucleic acids are the foundation of life. Most viruses, which are the simplest forms of life, contain only proteins and nucleic acids. Plants can produce their own complicated organic compound (food) needed for maintenance and continuation of their lives. They do this vital function through a process called photosynthesis. Overall, the existing life on earth is powered by solar energy. The green plants absorb the solar energy and, in their chloroplasts, convert it to chemical energy which will be finally stored in sugars and other organic molecules. During the whole process carbon dioxide in the air and water, which is usually absorbed from soil, combine to make organic compounds. For production of more complicated compounds, such as proteins, plants also absorb inorganic compounds such as, nitrogen salts from soil. The organic compounds produced by plants are directly or indirectly used by almost all living organisms on the earth. The foods produced by plants are directly used by herbivorous animals or indirectly by carnivorous animals. Human beings are omnivores, which, means they have the ability to consume both meat and plants. This fact shows that human beings are 100% dependent on plants and specific types of animals for their food. In other words, human beings should compete with each other and with other animals to obtain their foods. Later we will see that this fact is a very important factor in relations between human beings. It is obvious that we do not compete with other forms of life, which are not closely related to us. In competition for food, the main target of a human being is other human beings.

Foods used by all different types of living organisms are used for building the body and obtaining energy. All chemical compounds used by any sort of living organisms either directly or indirectly return to the "earth" The waste materials produced by a living organism or even the organism itself may be used by another organism in a series of contacts which overall is referred to as a food chain reaction. After death, the whole chemical components used in the body of any organism will finally return to the earth by gradual body decay. The returned chemicals, which are either in a very simple form or to a certain degree complicated are finally re-used by plants and the cycle initiates again. Nearly all major atoms which make our bodies go through such cycles. In a simple word, the same atoms used in any living organisms might have been used by many other organisms in the past and may be used by many other forms of life in the future. In other words, what makes our bodies belong to us only for a short period of time during our lives. After death, the same materials may even be used in the body of another human being. It seems during our life, through a very complicated process, we borrow certain atoms from the earth, use them for a short period of time and return them to the earth. It is obvious that during our lives in a series of reactions these atoms react with each other and give us "life". Death is a disruption in a very vital or a series of vital reactions, which in normal conditions happens in our bodies. What we call soul is nothing except well- organized reactions in the body. After death, for a short time, a number of these reactions may continue to take place, but real network coordination between all essential chemical reactions is needed for an active life.

There are over 2,000,000 different species of living organisms on the earth and mankind is one of them. This number does not include the extinct species. Of course, each species is divided into several strains and/or races. Different strains of one species are all the same with minor difference in certain genes. Overall, different species, which are genetically close to each other, belong to a genus; and close genera forms families. Generally, all 2,000,000 species are divided in three major groups (kingdoms) named Protista, plants, and animals. Protista are mostly microscopic organisms. A number of these microscopic organisms cause infectious diseases in other species including human beings; however, most of them are 100% essential for the presence of life on earth. It is the action of a number of these microorganisms that finally cause decay in the bodies of other advanced life. In other words, without the actions of these microorganisms, the life on the earth will not go through a cycle and finally will end. The variety in microorganisms is very interesting. They are nearly everywhere on the earth and their numbers in certain places are billions.

A group of them, which are generally named "algae", are responsible for the production of over 90% of foods on the earth. Most algae live in oceans. As noted above, plants are the second major group of life on earth. Overall, with a few exceptions, all plants can produce their own food. This is why they do not have real "active" movement. In other words, plants are mostly fixed in the soil. Although plants compete, their competition is very limited. Plants had major roles on the earth such as balance in the gases present in the atmosphere. Overall, existence of animals on the earth is directly or indirectly related to the existence of plants.

The third major types of life on the earth are animals. The simplest definition for this group is: They are always resting except when they are searching for food. In other words, food is the major issue for all animals. Of course, to a lower extent, a place to live and territory are the second and third major factors. Human beings are the most advanced type of animals. The subject of human behaviors will be discussed in more detail in the following pages; however, it worth mentioning that the human needs are more complicated than other animals.

With few exceptions, human beings can increase the numbers of certain other species and use them as nutrition. Obviously, any group of human beings who can perform such a task in the best possible way, has more advantages. To reach their goals, mankind needs specific tools and instruments which, directly or indirectly need energy for operation. Energy by itself is not enough to fulfill all other major needs of human beings. For production of food, good soil, water sources, good climates, and similar factors are also essential. This means that human beings are also looking for better places to live. There are many other minor factors related to the way that human beings live and behave. Overall, these major and minor factors directly or indirectly affect human beings and causes competition between them.

How life began on the earth? There are many scientific theories and non-scientific thoughts about how life was first formed. Of these theories and thoughts, three of them have been mostly the center of debates by different groups of people. The first non-scientific thought states that life started on the earth by a spontaneous arising controlled by a super power in a very short time. According to this thought, the intelligent designer or super power 'God" created our universe as a one-time event and during this event life was created. This thought is almost entirely based on religious beliefs and therefore it has more or less the same message in all major religions. Based on this belief the creation of all things happened in only several days. Of course, the existence of human beings has been the major subject for the followers of these beliefs and therefore they stated that Adam and Eve were the first man and woman on the earth. In other words, Adam and Eve are the grand grand parents of everybody. These people also believe that many years ago because of a worldwide flood nearly all sorts of life on the earth faced flood danger and therefore an individual named Noah tried to save life on the earth by making a ship to confront the flood.

Most followers of this thought believe that the earth is only ten thousand years old. Those who are supporting this type of creation believe that the religions and true science are in full harmony with each other. A major goal of the followers of this thought is to point out the weakness of the evolutionary theory. They emphasize on the creation as the correct answer to the existence of humans on earth. Overall, they are mostly interested in the creation of human beings and when they presented their ideas many years ago, they did not even know that beside human beings, 2,000,000 other species were also considered a part of life on earth. The occurrence of spontaneous generation was the subject of debates for several scientists even up to 19th century.

A number of scientists who were mainly interested in the science of microbiology thought that at least microorganisms are made from foods. They thought life could arise from something nonliving. Louis Pasteur, the most powerful opponent of the spontaneous generation, in 1864 proved that living organisms could not and cannot simply form from non-living matter. Can you imagine how something so complex (life) be formed spontaneously from nonliving things in a few days? So, it seems the idea of creation does not have any real scientific supports and therefore simply, is not acceptable. Needless to mention that nothing related to creation of life by a super power can be proven and there is no reliable evidence to support the idea.

The second theory related to the formation of life on the earth states that about 3-4 billion years ago some sort of simple life or even organic molecules that could finally produce life reached the earth by comets or meteorites. According to this theory, these molecules either directly reached the earth or first were on mars and then transferred to earth. Although this theory is more reliable than the previous one, there are a number of issues related to it that should be addressed.

As we already know, the physical conditions away from earth differ drastically with the physical conditions on earth. It is hard for life, as we know, to function for even a short period of time in the harsh physical conditions. The intensity of radiations and particles, even 100 kilometer above the earth, are so high that life cannot tolerate them. The cosmic rays have ionization properties and in a short time alter the genetic structure of any sort of life. We also know that the distances between planets and solar systems are so vast that it is not easy for any sort of life, even in a simple form, to easily travel and reach the earth. The hypothetical life should travel in a dark, cold, and full of harmful radiations environment to reach the earth. We may say that the harsh environment actually caused mutations in the life during its journey and what finally reached the earth has been the final refined form of life. Overall, movement of any sort of life in space is not so easy.

We will later discuss the problems associated with traveling in space in more detail. Even if we accept that life came to earth from another planet, one may ask how the same life was formed on a previous planet. We may say it went there from another planet that finally shows a chain transfer format. If we go back in time, we will finally reach a point at which life was formed "somewhere" in space. This means, that "somewhere" could be our planet. In other words, the earth is a good candidate on which life could originate.

The third theory states that life originated on the earth from some sort of "primordial soup" and in a prolonged process lifeless planet changed to a one filled with living things. Since this theory is based on scientific facts we will discuss it in more detail. This theory overall says that chemical reactions and physical processes on the early environment of the earth caused formation of life. Once the simple molecules associated with the life were developed, the simple molecules then transformed to more complicated sort of living things. It should be mentioned that chemical, physical, and geological studies support this theory. Most geologists believe that the earth began as a cold world that later melted from too much heat generated by internal compaction, radioactive decay, and possible impact by meteorites.

The first atmosphere on the earth was mostly composed of hydrogen gas. Gradually, during time, geological events especially volcanoes released other types of gases in the atmosphere of early earth and formed a new atmosphere consists of water vapor, carbon monoxide, methane, ammonia, and hydrogen. The condensation of water in the atmosphere and gradual cooling caused too much rain and huge water reservoirs were formed. Presence of water, certain gases, intense radiations (especially ultraviolet radiation), heat, lightning, and volcanic activity caused production of simple molecules associated with the life. Life as we know it now is in fact continuum extending from earliest simple organisms formed on the earth. In the following pages we will survey the diversity and complexity of life and trace the evolution in life.

In this chapter we only briefly explain the effect of evolution on earth's environment. As an example, oxygen, which is a very vital gas for living organisms, was released in the early stages of the earth's history by biological functions of photosynthetic organisms. Historical and scientific studies on past records revealed the structure of the earth in the early stages. Obviously, studies on early fossils helped us to simply understand the diversity in the life on the early earth. Studies on early Precambrian fossils show that some sorts of microorganisms were living on the earth about 3.5 billion years ago in an area, which is now Australia. This means that a simpler form of life should have existed on earth in an earlier time. It seems sometimes around 4.1 billion years ago the first molecules associated with life were formed.

The scientists who studied the origin of life on the earth believe that life on the earth developed from nonliving materials. These materials first produced simple molecules and later the aggregation in these molecules finally ended to the molecules, which could self-replicate. People who oppose this theory ask why this event does not happen in today's earth. The answer to this question is simple. We are talking about earth when it was only one billion years old. The biologists who are supporting the hypothesis associated to the formation of life on the earth believe that life on early earth was shaped in four continuous stages; (1) in the first stage, small organic molecules such as amino acids (building structure of proteins) and nucleotides (building structure of nucleic acids) were formed; (2) gradual polymerization of small molecules produced proteins and nucleic acids. Proteins and nucleic acids are the most important molecules associated with life on earth. Most viruses are only made of proteins and nucleic acids; (3) the aggregation of molecules formed in the previous stage finally produced droplet molecules which were different from their own surrounding media; (4) the droplets started replication and life started with the ability of replication of complicated molecules. How do we prove that these hypothetical events that happened 4 billion years ago are true?

In the 1920s, A. I. Oparin in Russia and J.B.S. Haldane in England conducted a series of experiments and postulated the early physical and chemical conditions on early earth. They were able to show that several chemical reactions, which cannot simply take place in the modern world, could happen in the early stages of earth. These reactions, which mainly took place in seas, produced organic compounds. Because of specific structure of atmosphere in the early earth and lack of oxygen, the small molecules gradually produced more complex ones. In the presence of lightning and ultraviolet radiations, which were energy sources, the atmosphere underwent changes and bigger molecules were formed. In 1953, S. Miller and H. Urey tested the Oparin—Haldane theory and in the laboratory under conditions similar to the early earth, could make amino acids and other organic compounds found in the today's living organisms. In the experiments conducted by Miller and Urey the same gases, which were present in ancient world, were present. After performing these simple experiments, gradually in different laboratories, using the primeval earth condition, scientists made 20 amino acids, several sugars, lipids, bases present in DNA and RNA and even ATP in the presence of phosphate compounds. It is obvious that early life on earth has been very simple. The heredity originated when the simple aggregated molecules could pass genetic information.

Although there are many debates about the origin of life on earth, whatever way life originated on earth, the production of a group of chemical compounds enclosed with a membrane compartment on the early earth was certain. Such packed molecules, which could replicate their genetic programs and metabolize organic compounds, were early living cells. At present we know that all kingdoms of life descended from these early cells, which were on the earth about 3.5 billion years ago. Geological studies revealed that life originated about 4000 million years ago. In about 2500 million years ago photosynthetic microorganism caused accumulation of oxygen in the atmosphere. Early eukaryotic cells were formed in close to 1500 million years ago, followed by formation of multi-cellular organisms in close to 500 million years ago. Plants and dinosaurs were colonized on land about 300 million years ago. First humans were originated about 2 million years ago. Humans with relatively advanced knowledge are only about 30,000 years old. Above episodes, which are the main evolutionary process, will be discussed in more detail in the following pages.

What is a cell? The cell is fundamental of biology. All living organisms are either one cell or are made up of a group of cells. In other words, a cell is the simplest collection of matter which can have living functions. In biology, viruses are not considered real cells. Viruses can perform all living functions with the help of other more advanced cells. The bodies of most microorganisms consist of a single cell, which is able to complete the main functions of life, including exchange of materials and energy with surrounding environment, reproduction, and movement. The bodies of more advanced forms of living organisms including humans are made of billions of cells. In advanced organisms, a group of cells are specialized for a certain function; however, in a normal condition each cell can perform its own biological functions. A group of cells, which are all responsible for a specific function, are named tissue. Tissues form organs and a combination of several organs make a system (example, digestive system). Organized relations between systems make a complete multi-cellular organism. Though, to some extent, all cells are related by their descent form of earlier cells, they have been modified to live in different environments. Cells are relatively very small. The smallest cells are 0.1- 1.0 micrometer and the largest ones are about 10-100 micrometer in diameter. All cells have a boundary that is called membrane. In addition to the membrane, plant cells have an outer layer, which is called cell wall. Because of the cell wall, plant cells have a relatively fixed structure. The cell membrane serves as a partition and separate internal components of the cell, which is generally named cytoplasm, from the outside environment. All advanced cells have an internal body called the nucleus. The nucleus is covered by another membrane and contains most of the genetic information. The prokaryotic cells (example bacteria) have no true nucleus. In these cells genetic materials are released in the cytoplasm. Each cell has several additional specialized organelles. A number of these organelles are specific to plant cells and a group of them are found only in the animal cells. Explanation of structures and functions of the organelles is out of the limit of this book. Since in the following pages we may refer to a number of these organelles, in this section we only name them. They are: Golgi apparatus, lysosome, ribosomes, centrioles, microbody, microfilaments, mitochondria, flagellum, endoplasmic reticulum, vacuole, tonoplast, plasmodesmata, and chloroplast.

For normal function, each cell should obtain certain chemicals, which are generally named "food" from surrounding environments. Single cells (example bacteria) perform all biological functions and when they reach a certain size they divide and produce new cells. In other words, a bacterium never dies if all physical and chemical factors, which support its life, are provided. With a hypothetical calculation, we can predict that a bacterium with a generation time of 20 minutes will occupy the whole universe in few months in a suitable condition. This is not true with multi-cellular organisms. As discussed above, in advanced forms of life, such as human beings, different organs are responsible for various duties. For example, the heart pumps blood, which contains food and oxygen and sending it to different sections of the body. If for any reason this vital organ stops its function, the organism cannot properly function and therefore is considered dead. The death of a multi-cellular organism does not necessarily mean that all cells and tissues in the body are dead. For example, it is possible to use certain organs of a dead human being in the body of another human being provided that the transplant is performed in a short time. We will get back to this subject in the following pages. All multi-cellular organisms will finally die because of many different reasons. A number of these reasons are related to the environment. If we keep a human being in the best possible condition, it is still impossible to maintain this human being forever. The reason is the internal genetic information, which causes aging in the human. There is much advanced progress in preventing the aging process but it seems we will never be able to keep a "man" alive for a very long time. This subject is briefly discussed in this section to show that traveling out of our solar system is not an easy task. We will get back to this subject in the following pages.

One of the main functions of any living organism is reproduction. In other words, life arises only from existing life. The ability of any organism to reproduce their kind is the best phenomenon showing differences between living and non-living matter. The reproduction of a cell is based on cell division. In some cases, division of a cell produces an entire new cell; however, cell division may also enable multi-cellular organisms to grow from a single cell. It is obvious that division in a cell is not a simple process. Cell division must be associated with transfer of genetic materials (DNA). The total genetic material in the cell is named genome. The genome consists of one or several DNA molecules. Along the length of DNA molecules, thousands of genes are arranged in specific order. The genes and their order specify the organism's traits. Compact coiling and folding of DNA molecules is called chromosomes. The number of chromosomes in the cells is specific for each species (For example human has 23 pair or 46 single). Chromosomes are in the nucleus of the cells. A cell, which is ready to divide, should first copy all its genes and then equally transfer a copy of genetic material to the newly made cell. The process of cell division is very complicated. In this section we only discuss the subjects, which are relevant to our work.

There are two modes of reproduction. Asexual reproduction occurs when a single organism produces an offspring genetically like itself. Reproduction in most one--cell organisms are relatively simple and are called binary fission. This type of reproduction is asexual because one cell is enough to produce another cell. In sexual reproduction two individuals (male and female) are needed to produce offspring that of course has genetic information from both parents. This means that in one stage of reproduction in sexual reproduction, both parties should lose one pair of their genetic information (chromosomes) before two cells from both genders produce the zygote that contains two pairs of chromosomes. Example, all cells in human bodies, except sperm cells (male) and egg cell (female) have 46 chromosomes. During sexual reproduction the sperm cell and the egg cell (gametes) which each have 23 chromosomes combine to form a zygote which has 46 chromosomes; 23 from each parent. The zygote then starts serial divisions and produces thousands of cells. These cells then gradually differentiate and produce million of cells organized in tissues, organs, and systems and finally a new offspring (in identical twins one zygote produces two similar individuals) is born. Explanation of cell division and details of offspring formation are out of the limit of this book.

During both asexual and sexual reproduction, sometimes for different reasons the genetic makeup of offspring alters and the structure of chromosomes changes. I this case, the offspring either gain new character(s) or lose character(s), which normally should have. This phenomenon is generally called mutation. Mutation is very important in the evolution of life on the earth and therefore it will be discussed in more details. To understand mutations, we should first learn about DNA and genes.

What is DNA? DNA is the genetic material and it is one of the main components of life on the earth. All living organism (except a number of viruses which their genetic material is RNA) have DNA. Heredity information is encoded in the chemical language of DNA and it is this DNA program, which finally through production of specific proteins directs the development of biochemical, anatomical, physiological and to some extent behavioral traits in living organisms. Today, we can alter DNA and artificially cause changes in the genetic information of living organisms. This process is generally called genetic engineering and as we know it has had many influences in the life on the earth. The discovery of DNA and its relation with heredity go back to Mendel works. Gregor Mendel (1822-1884), an Austrian monk, discovered the basic principles of heredity by breeding garden peas in a series of carefully planned experiments. Of course, during Mendel's time scientists did not know anything about DNA but Mendel's conclusions have become the basic tenets of genetics and a notable influence on later works. Thomas H. Morgan, (1866–1945), an American zoologist worked on Mendel's ideas and discovered the physical basis of heredity and the importance of the genes. He described the phenomena of linkage and crossing over, which later he and his students utilized to map the linear arrangement of genes along the chromosome. Subsequent works by many scientists confirmed that DNA is the genetic material and the foundation of life. The overall molecular structure of DNA was discovered by James Watson and Francis Crick in1953.

DNA consists of many subunits which each is called a nucleotide. In other words, nucleotides arranged in a specific chain make the DNA. Each nucleotide consists of a nitrogenous base {Four different bases are used in the structure of DNA; they are named: Thymine (T), Adenine (A), Cytosine (C), and Guanine (G)}, a molecule of sugar (deoxyribose), and a phosphate group}. In RNA sugar is ribose and Uracil (U) is found instead of Thymine. There are only four types of nucleotides and 20 different types of amino acids. Each three nucleotides specify one amino acid. Example, AAC specifies amino acid Trp, AAA specifies amino acid Phe, and CCG specify amino acid Gly. In this example, a section of DNA with the base sequence of AAC AAA CCG produces a protein with the following amino acids in a sequence: Trp-Phe-Gly. In other words, the maintenance of exact chain arrangement of nucleotides on the DNA molecules is very important in constant transfer of genetic materials. A number of nucleotides that occupy certain section of DNA make a gene and each gene is responsible for a certain character. Each gene has a specific sequence of bases. Genes are the instructions for making specific proteins. They do not directly build the proteins. Genes transfer their information through RNA in a series of very complicated processes and finally different proteins are made in the cells. Proteins are in fact the molecules which control nearly all body functions. Proteins consist of 20 amino acids arranged in certain chains governed by certain genes on DNA of chromosomes. It is obvious that a minor change in even one base in a nucleotide lead to a change in the sequence of amino acids in the protein. In other words, change in the molecular structure of a protein may change a specific cell function and finally may change a specific character in the organism.

What is a mutation? Any changes in the genetic makeup in any living organism are called mutations and any factors that can cause these changes are called mutagens. Mutations can also be defined as an alteration in structure of chromosomes. Mutation is sometimes a minor change and therefore it is called point mutation. In point mutation the chemical structure of one or few nucleotides in a single gene change. A number of chemical and physical agents can cause this type of mutation. As we already know, radiations can ionize atoms and remove electron in the atoms. DNA is made of atoms. This means, if an organism is exposed to high dosage of a certain radiation; the radiation may cause changes in the chemical bounds and alter the DNA chemical structure. Example, imagine that the sequence of bases in a hypothetical gene is: TAT TCG GGC TAC TTC AAC .... Now imagine that due to damage in this gene one **C** is detached from the sequence. The resulting sequence then will be TAT TCG GGC TAT TCA AC....In this example, due to a minor change in the sequence of bases in a gene, a different protein will be made.

Radiations such as alpha $^{++}$, beta$^-$, and gamma, which are emitted from decays in the radioactive atoms, X-ray, and particles such as proton and neutron can cause damages in the DNA structure. This means that, in the laboratory we can change the genetic structure of an organism by using these radiations.

If a point mutation occurs in the male or female gametes. It may be transmitted to offspring and subsequently to the following generations. Overall, this type of change in the DNA is called genetic disorder, or heredity disease. Later we will see that such a change is not always a "disease". Mutations are not always so minor. Sometimes a piece of DNA detaches from the whole DNA molecule. Sometimes the detached piece attaches to the same section of DNA in the inverted shape. In some cases the same piece attachés to another section of the same DNA molecule or another DNA molecule. There are cases in that a piece of a chromosome attaches to another chromosome. Sometimes during formation of a gamete, an extra chromosome enters the gamete, or a gamete may loose a chromosome. So, we now know that changes in the genetic structure of a cell can happen by different methods. We also now that any changes in the genetic structure of a cell can be transferred to offspring.

It is obvious that mutations cause changes in the character(s) of offspring. It is also obvious that any changes in the normal properties of any organisms are bad and usually offspring that differ from its parent are considered abnormal. It may be true if we call such an offspring an abnormal individual. Mutations differ from each other by the degree of changes in the offspring. It is obvious that a drastic change in the offspring may even cause death in the offspring due to lack of many genes. On the other hand, a minor change may cause loss of a character or even occurrence of a new character. Overall, most mutations are called "negative" mutations because offspring loses some character and therefore cannot live; however, in rare cases, a mutation may produce a new character which can be very useful and therefore is considered a positive mutation.

Example: **imagine** that in a hypothetical population who were all exposed to an atomic bomb many different types of genetic changes happened in all members of the population. Also imagine that all these individuals transfer their genetic materials to their children. It is obvious that different kids with different disabilities will be born. Those kids who have major and drastic abnormality will sooner or later die. Now imagine that one kid out of thousands of mutated kids gain a character, which is very important for survival and makes him even better than his own parents. Obviously, this kid with such a new important character will have a better opportunity in the population. It should be noted that changes in offspring due to mutations may sometimes be unpleasant for us but this does not mean that the change is not useful. For example, imagine in a hypothetical population, due to a mutation, a person with four hands is born. For all other individuals in such a hypothetical population having four hands is an abnormal condition. What about the mutated person himself? For him having four hands is actually an advantage. This person, with four hands can do the job of two normal individuals who each has only two hands. In such a population this person is always in a fight with others. Later we will see that these types of changes and behaviors may lead to evolution.

Mutations happen naturally but we can increase their rates. Artificial induction of mutation solved a number of our problems. In agriculture, production of better crops is the results of artificial changes in the genetic structure of certain plants. Overall, the term "genetic engineering" is associated with these changes. Natural mutations may happen in any organism at any time. Several factors, such as cosmic rays, may cause natural mutations in an organism. The possibility of a change may be rare but it may happen.

In this chapter, the earth, its composition in early dates, and the origin of life on the earth were discussed. Briefly, the diversity of life and general structure of living matter were explained. Also, in the simplest possible way, the structure of a cell, its genetic material, and the mechanisms of mutations were explained.

CHAPTER FOUR

Mechanisms of evolution, and The Origin of Species

Writing about religions and evolution are probably the most difficult part of this book. It is difficult because, during the history of mankind a group of people simply accepted a certain belief and based on their belief; oppose any idea, which differs from their own ideas. It is obvious that changing the minds of these people is almost impossible. Nevertheless, presenting scientific facts and reliable data regarding these subjects is the duty of any individuals who believe in the advancement of human beings. I personally think that those who oppose evolution either do not understand it or they may believe in evolution but cannot accept it due to religious reasons. For these individuals, in chapter three to five the mechanisms of evolution, origin of species and evolution of mankind are explained in the easiest possible way.

The science of biology changed when in 1859 Charles Darwin (1809-1882) published " the origin of species by means of natural selection". In his book, Darwin presented convincing data and showed that diverse life on earth has been transformed from the earliest form of life in the process of evolution. The main idea was about the diversity of the organisms, the origin and relationship between different forms of life, similarities and differences between organisms, adaptations, and geographic distribution. A number of these topics were not main subjects in biology at that time and could be explained only by evolution. Darwin insisted on two points: (1) he showed that different species were not created by their present form and were evolved from ancestral species, and (2) he proposed a mechanism for evolution and named it natural selection. Darwin defined the natural selection as a process by which a change in population occurs because of the increase in the numbers of offspring in this population compared with another population. The evolutionary changes are based on relations and interactions between organisms and their environments. The Darwin's idea at the time contradicted the views of those who believed in creation of life and thought that the earth is only about 10 thousand years old. Before Darwin people mostly believed Greek philosophers who ruled out evolution. Aristotle (384-322 B.C.) thought that the species are fixed and do not evolve. The idea that God created life, presented by major religions, was also against evolution. Before Darwin none of the scientists of the time could topple the doctrine of fixed species. In the 18th century, Carolus Linnaeus (1707-1778), published the diversity in life and tried to classify similar species in a group. Linnaeus found order in the diversity of life but believed that species were permanent creations. Interestingly, Darwin with a century to explain the evolution used the idea of Linnaeus later. For better understanding about the diversity between species, study on fossils is very important. Fossils are impressions of organisms, which were living in the past. Fossil records are very useful evidence showing the link between organisms in the past and present. Scientific observation of fossils by Georges Cuvier (1769 -1832) showed the extinction of several species that were living on earth in the past. Cuvier believed that after extinction of certain species, which could be due to many different reasons such as environmental catastrophes, new species replace them. Even before Darwin, several naturalists including Jean B. Lamarck (1744-1829) suggested evolution. By study on fossils, Lamarck noticed that old species lead to modern species. Lamarck had two ideas, (1) environment has a major role in changing the characters, and (2) the modification of an organism acquired during its life can be passed to its offspring. Although Lamarck first idea could have some scientific support, his second idea was not right. We now know that only changes in the genetic structure of organisms can be transferred to offspring.

While only 22 years old (1831) Darwin sailed from England and went to the South American coastline. In there, he collected many species and found the unique adaptation of organisms to their environments. He also noticed the geographic distribution of species. Darwin realized that the origin of species and adaptation are two processes, which are closely related. Darwin suggested that a new species would arise from previous species by the gradual accumulation of adaptation to various environmental conditions. He also suggested that geographic barriers and adaptation to local conditions, gradually and over generations are enough to separate species. Darwin thought that once changes take place, because of natural selection, evolution took place. Based on his idea, distribution of organisms into various habitats over millions of years and adaptations caused accumulation of diverse modifications in organisms and consequently fit them to specific ways of life. In the Darwinian view, the history of life is like a tree. All organisms came from a trunk and branches are a new organism; obviously the most recent ones are on the tips. In other words, species that are closely related (example, dog and wolf) share many characteristics because they belong to the smallest branches of the tree of life.

To understand the origin of species, we should know that the individuals of a species become better adapted to their local environment through natural selection. The logic of natural selection is based on several facts including, (1) All species have the ability to reproduce and increase their population, (2) Most populations are stable in size, (3) Natural resources including food, and space for living is limited, therefore only a small number of offspring survive in each generation, (4) Production of more individuals in a limited space leads to struggle (fight for survival), (5) Individuals in a population have their own characteristics and these characteristics are heritable. This means that the struggle for existence is not a random phenomenon, but it depends on the ability of each individual for survival. Only those individuals who have characteristics which best fit with their environments can survive and consequently increase their offspring, (6) The ability of individuals to survive and increase in the number of their offspring finally ends to gradual change in the population and gradual accumulation of favorable characteristics. The outcome of natural selection is the survival of species, which could best adapt themselves to the environment conditions through adaptation.

As discussed in the previous chapter, populations are subjected to variations and variations in populations of species can happen through mutations and genetic recombination. An organism that through genetic changes gained new characteristics can survive only if this organism is able to adapt itself to the environment and increase its population by transferring new characteristics to the offspring. Obviously, during this process, struggle for life (fight for survival) is ensured by increasing the population size of new individuals.

T. Malthus in 1798 noted that most of human suffering such as famine, diseases, wars, and homelessness are the results of increase in human population when the food supply is limited. This fact is true with nearly all species and is actually the main factor for maintenance of population size in all organisms. Later we will see that at present human beings are not exactly following this natural phenomenon. For example, improvement in the living conditions and advancement in the medicine caused increase in the life expectancy (increase in the population) of humans to a degree, which is not proportional to the food supply. We will also discuss about other factors, which influence human population. These factors (for example, energy needed for survival) have not been an issue at the time of Malthus. In other words, in each generation of human only those who can best adapt themselves and the variations in the environment is in their favor, have a better chance for survival. This means that humans are always in fight for the best.

The process of changes in the species and natural section has been scientifically proven. The results of scientific evidence are new breeding of domesticated animals and plants. If we summarize Darwin's idea, we will see that the diverse forms of life (including human) are the result of accumulated modifications obtained from previous forms of life. While discussing about human evolution, we will see that at present time, human evolution seems not be following the natural way. It should be noted that natural selection involves interaction between organisms and their environment. Evolution is not a process taking place in a very short time. If fact, it is a process which takes place over a long period of time. In other words, an organism may be able to adapt itself to a new environment, but this does not mean that this organism evolves. It should also be emphasized that evolution in species left many observable signs in the earth and many aspects of evolution can be proven by scientific experiments. Explaining the details of this scientific data is out of the limit of this book. Nonetheless, we should briefly discuss several scientific facts, which are needed for better understanding of human evolution.

During the evolution process, new and modern species evolve in a region from ancestors that inhabited in the same region. The newly formed species increase their population in the same region and usually have certain geographic distribution. To understand the distribution of life on earth in the past, studies on fossil records are very important because these studies scientifically show us the relation between species. For example, many recent functions of advanced living organisms, such as biochemical, molecular, and overall biological properties, are like those of simple organisms which have been living on earth from billions of years ago. Another example is taxonomical relations between organisms. For example, scientific observations show that fishes predate all other vertebrates, with amphibians next, followed by reptiles, mammals, and birds. A good example supporting the above fact is the study on skulls shape and size of mammals, which prove close relation between them and confirm that mammals evolved from reptiles.

Evolution can also be better understood if we study anatomical similarities between the species, which are all in the same taxonomic category. For example, the skeletal elements in appendages of humans, dogs, bats, and whales, which are all mammals, are similar however, they are different species. These appendages, according to the need, have different shapes. Comparative anatomy showed that modification in the appendages took place because they needed to perform new and different functions.

Comparative embryology is another tool, which helps us to better understand evolution. All closely related organisms follow similar stages in their embryonic development process. For example, all vertebrate embryos, including human, in a stage of embryonic development go through a stage of having gill, which is a characteristic of the fishes. In fact, during embryonic development, the similarity between fishes, frogs, lizards, birds, humans and other vertebrates are more than their differences. It should be noted that similarity between the species does not necessarily mean that an organism can easily change to another one. For example, embryonic similarities do not mean that during embryonic stages a human is first fish and then becomes frog and finally change to human. Comparative embryology is mostly useful to establish structural similarities between closely related species.

Recent advancement in scientific investigation proved evolution in the molecular levels. The most important sign of evolution at the molecular level is the properties of DNA and protein synthesis. In other words, if two species have a similar protein, this means that this protein in both species was copied from a similar gene and therefore the two species have the same gene. Likewise, similarity between more characters has a direct correlation with closer relations. For example, human and bacteria perform biochemical pathways of respiration in more or less a similar way. This means that we are related to bacteria; however, our relation to chimpanzee is closer than to that of bacteria because the number of similarities between human and chimpanzee is more than human and bacteria. Having similar genes means close evolutionary relations.

Simply it is shown that genetically all sort of life on earth are following a common genetic process and genetic codes in them proved that they are related. Thus, the data collected by molecular biology studies are the final and most supporting evidence that confirm evolution as the basis of diversity in life. It also showed that humans are closely related to other organisms on earth and are not a separate category of life. Some people argue and emphasize that Darwin's ideas about evolution are only a "theory". We already discussed that most of the evolutionary process can be scientifically proven by experimental studies.

We now have a general idea about the evolution process and therefore continue to talk about effects of evolution on the population of species. Changes in the genetic components of an organism cause formation of a new organism. Natural selection affects survival of such organism. If the newly formed organism is able to adapt itself to the new environment (adaptation may involve struggle for survival) it will survive. In fact, it is not the organism, which evolved, but rather it is the population formed from this organism through reproduction, which evolve. We go back to the hypothetical example in the previous chapter. In the previous chapter, in a hypothetical example, we assumed that by a genetic mistake a person with four hands is born. This hypothetical person will have a life and after certain years will die. In other words, this person did not evolve and nothing drastic happened in its population. However, if the same person, due to a new characteristic which is better than the previous ones (four hands versus two hands) can transfer his genetic materials and increase his population, then we can say that the new population is in the process of evolution. Needless to mention that in our example, the newly formed population, which its entire member now has four hands, have a better opportunity to live. They can perform their daily activities faster and gradually due to competition replace the previous population that in fact has been its own ancestor. The above hypothetical example has been proven many times in different organisms. The simplest example is the resistance of certain microorganisms to certain antibiotic; an evolutionary process, which is taking place due to the natural selection. In this process, many microorganisms become resistance to antibiotics. Overall, the above information shows that all species including *Homo sapiens* (human) are the products of evolution.

In recent years, with the birth of population genetics, the theory of evolution is better explained and understood. A population is a group of more or less similar individuals belonging to one species. In a population, each member of the group (except identical twins) has its own genetic structure. However, overall similarity between genetic components of the individuals belonging to one species is more than the same similarity between two close species. Generally, each species has a geographic range and the members of a species are usually localized. As we will see later this is not exactly true with human. The genetic exchange between the members of one species is possible; however, two populations of one species may also rarely exchange genetic material. Populations are not necessarily isolated and therefore they do not necessarily have sharp boundaries.

Later we will see that humans actually try to make a boundary and usually fight to keep this boundary (borders). A population that gets highly populated may move into another immediate region and mix with another population. This is one of the main reasons which animals, including humans, get involved in wars. Also, if a species is populated and have enough power, this species may move to the territory of another species which is less numerous and have less power. This is also something, which humans are doing and we will discuss it later. One of the most important characteristics of all species is the sexual relation between the members of the same species. Because of specific genetic components (example the same number of chromosomes in the male and female), and other characteristics, such as physiological, anatomical, and overall structural similarities, the members of a species can have sex and genetic exchange only with their own mate.

As noted in the introduction section, the main aim of this book is reviewing the human origin, behavior, and future. For better understanding of above subjects, an attempt has been made to explain scientific facts in the easiest possible language. Since the subject of human evolution is an important part of this book, more information regarding this subject will be presented here. It is obvious that any subject discussed in this book can be better explained if we present more scientific data. This approach is out of the limit of this book therefore information presented here is only briefly reviewed.

Overall, evolution in a population involves changes in the genetic structure, increase in the number of individuals whose genetic material is altered, struggle for existence and natural selection. In fact, natural selection accumulates and maintains favorable genes in the population. We should emphasize that not all changes in a population is heritable and therefore ends to evolution. Only changes in the genetic structure of organisms are heritable. As discussed before, one of the factors causing variation in genetic materials is mutation. Mutations happen in all genes in all living organisms and at different rates. This means that the frequency of mutation in a number of genes maybe more than others. It is also important to know that most of mutations are lethal and only those that happen in the gametes can be transferred to offspring. Changes in the genetic material may also take place due to other reasons such as, random genetic drift and gene flow and migration. Of these reasons, the most important one is alteration in the chromosome in the cells, which can happen by many different methods.

Now which we have a general idea about evolution, we will briefly discuss the origin of the species. When we talk about "species" we mean one kind of living organism. For example, dogs, horses, humans, wheat, apple, and iris are all species of living organisms.

In other words, species exist in the nature as discrete biological units. Each species consists of several strains, example there are many different strains of dogs. Because of many genetic determinants, usually a member of one species live close to each other and through sexual relation, transfer their genetic materials to their own offspring. In other words, a biological species is a population of a group of individuals whose members have the potential to transfer their genes to their offspring.

One of the most important features of species is their physical appearance. All member of a species has more or less the same shape; however, they are each one unit of life and have their own genetic material. For example, all humans have the same shape but, except the identical twins, each one has its own genetic material. We should make it clear that the shape by itself does not determine the species. For example, humans and chimpanzees have similar shape but remain distinct species because they cannot interbreed. It is also useful to mention that species are defined by their reproductive behavior in the nature. In an artificial environment, such as a laboratory, it is possible to exchange genetic components between species that do not interbreed in the nature. We should also remember that transfer of genetic material is not necessarily sexual.

A significant number of species transfer their genetic materials to their offspring through asexual reproduction.

The genetic changes in the organisms, which may finally lead to evolution and formation of new organisms, are not always confined to a small number of genes. The evolution may take place as a "macroevolution". In other words, sometimes evolution causes genetic changes, which are substantial enough to produce new genera or family of organisms. For example, mammals originated from reptiles. However, these two groups of organisms belong to two different classes of organisms; investigations show that in a stage of evolution in the life, one evolves from another. It is obvious that macroevolution happens when drastic environmental changes take place. For example, it is believed that mammals appeared following the disappearance of dinosaurs. One may ask, how scientists reached such a conclusion. The answer is extensive studies performed on the fossils. Fossils are the historical documents of biology and are considered the best scientific tools, which can be used to study the structure of life in the past. They are formed when dead organisms captured in sediments, decayed and left empty molds which later become filled with minerals. It should be noted that the sedimentary fossils are not the only kind of fossils. If an organism dies in a place and for any reason bacteria and fungi do not decompose its body, the organism may remain intact for many years and become a fossil. A mammoth that remained in the Arctic ice for a long time is a good example of these types of fossils. If we determine their ages, fossils are the most reliable historical tools. Now you may ask how we know the ages of fossils. The relative dating of fossils can be estimated by finding the date of the layer of sediment in which the fossils were formed. The absolute ages of fossils can be calculated by radioactive dating of the fossils. Radioactive atoms are isotopes of atoms which, depending on the atoms, emit radiations (gamma, alpha, or beta). Example carbon—14 (radioisotope of carbon-12, emits beta radiation). Because each radioactive isotope has a fixed rate of decay, it can be used to determine the age of sediments that contain the radioisotopes. The half-life of a radioisotope is the time that takes for 50% of the original radioisotope to decay. Example, the half-life of carbon -14 is 5600 years. This means that if a sample has 1000 of carbon-14, after 5600 years the numbers of carbon-14 in this sample will be 500. Obviously, the number of remaining carbons-14 will be 250 after 11200 years. Fossils contain radioisotopes of elements that accumulated in the organisms when they were alive. Therefore, with the knowledge of half-life of an element that exists in the fossil, one can determine the age of the fossil. It should be noted that carbon- 14 dating is mostly used for relatively young fossils and is a very important tool for archeologists. Radioisotopes with longer half-life are used for dating of the old fossils. By studying on fossils, one can trace the cause of large- scale evolution in the organisms.

For example, studies performed on fossils showed that birds were evolved from dinosaurs. Another example, human brains are relatively larger than chimpanzee brains because growth of the organ is switched off later in human development. One most influencing factor in the macroevolution is biogeography events. Drift in continents and movement of organisms from oceans to lands have a major effect on their evolution. Geological events also played major roles in the evolution of organisms. For example, massive geological events caused mass extinction of a number of species and formation of the new species. In other words, evolutionary changes in one species had impact on other species. Studies showed that many species, which were on the earth before, have disappeared and new species replaced them. This means that there is a possibility that human species one day in the future may disappear. We will get back to this subject later. Regarding the effect of geological events on the evolution, investigations showed that about 65 million years ago nearly half of the organisms on the earth including the dinosaurs disappeared (The Cretaceous Crisis). It is shown that an asteroid crashing into the earth about 65 million years ago caused the 180-kilometer- wide crater located in the Yucatan coat of Mexico. Research showed that extinctions of many species at about 65 million years ago are related to this impact. The species that managed to survive such a drastic geological event gradually adapted themselves with the new environment and ended to form new species. It is believed that the evolution of humans has root in the same impact. Using new methods facilitated study on the relations between past and present species at the level of molecules. By applying newly developed methods, such as PCR (Polymerase Chain Reactions), scientists could analyze the DNA samples of past living organisms and compare it with the DNA structure of the present species.

In chapter four, briefly we reviewed the mechanisms of the evolution, and the origin of the species. By presenting scientific data and reliable examples, we could show that evolution is a biological process and it is the major cause of changes in the species. Evolution takes place when a change in genetic structure of a species is transferred to its offspring. The ability of such an offspring to increase the population is the major factor for formation of a new organism. We also noted that the struggle for existence and natural selections play a major role in evolution. In this chapter we also explained the effect of major geological events on extinction of a number of species and appearances of new species. In the following chapter we review the diversity in animals and evolution of humans.

CHAPTER FIVE

Animal Diversity and
Evolution of Human

The subject of this book is mainly focused on the existence of humans on earth, their origin, relations and future. Since there is a close relation between humans and animals, when appropriate, subjects related to animals will be discussed with those of human. In other words, biology of other animals will be discussed only when it is needed.

Animal life on earth started in the early seas with the evolution of multi-cellular organisms, which could eat other organisms. This means that one of the most important features of all animals is eating other form of life. This also means that animals need some sort of active movement to find their own foods. Since the majority of plants make their own food and are the first groups of organisms in food chain, they mostly do not have active movement and therefore are usually fixed somewhere on the earth. As we know, algae present in the oceans and seas also make their own food and are the main producer of the food in the oceans. Most algae are not fixed and are always in movement according to the movement of the water in which they live. Movement of animals in the early stages of animal formation led to an evolutionary change in the life and formation of new and diverse species. Early animals were in the water and gradually new species moved to the land. This transfer took place nearly 700 million years ago and the animals which now exist on the earth (including humans) are the result of many years of evolution. There are several phyla of animals but we only emphasize on vertebrates, which are mostly related to humans. Vertebrates consist of fishes, amphibians, reptilians, birds and mammals. These animals, all together are only 5% of total animal species. In this chapter the origin of early animals including humans will be discussed.

It is not easy to define animals but generally speaking, (1) animals are multi-cellular organisms which have the ability of ingestion, (2) they can store glycogen in contrast to plants which store starch, (3) their cells lack cell walls, (4) they have nerve and muscle tissues used for movement, and (5) they mostly reproduce sexually. Above characteristics show that animals are always in a struggle to find their food for living and continuation of their generation. Later we will see that this is one the main problems of humans at the present time.

It seems early animals were derived from protista and gradually invertebrates which consists of many different types invertebrate animals such as jellyfish, flatworms, round worms, clams, insects, etc. were formed. Even a short description about these animals is out of the limit of this book. Here, we only mention that arthropods (insects, spiders, crustaceans) have a population of about 10^{18} individuals and they consist of more than 1/2 of all species on earth.

Arthropods are the most successful types of animals that have ever lived on earth. What about humans? We will discuss it later.

Studies on fossils found in Canada showed that the vertebrate animals originated about 550 million years ago. Vertebrates have internal skeleton and most of them possess well-developed sense organs associated with their brains. Since the majority of them have a column shape skeletal unit, they are called "vertebrates". Male and female are separate in most vertebrates. In this group of animals, fishes live in the water. Amphibians generally live either in water or on the land. A group of reptiles live in the water but have several adaptations for terrestrial living. Birds and mammals have groups which can have living activities in the water, land and air. Since mammals originated from reptiles, briefly we will discuss them. Reptiles are a diverse group of animals and today represent about 7000 species. The oldest reptilian fossils are found in the rocks from 300 million years ago. They were evolved from amphibians. The first major groups of terrestrial reptiles were predators. Among these groups of reptiles, a smaller subgroup named "therapsids" was a mammal-like organism and it is believed that mammals, including humans, originated from this subgroup. The early therapsids were dog-size predators. Another group of reptiles, thecodonts, were ancestors of dinosaurs. Dinosaurs originated about 200 million years ago. They were extremely diverse with different body shape and size. The largest animals to ever inhabit the land belonged to this group of animals. Fossils recently found in the New Mexico showed that a number of dinosaurs weighed about 100 tons. As discussed before, about 65 million years ago and in a period of about 5-10 million years the dinosaurs disappeared (The Cretaceous Crisis) from the earth and their extinction originated appearance of mammals, which is dated to about 60 million years ago.

Mammals and on the top of them humans are considered the most advanced form of life on the earth. Today, there are about 4500 species of mammals on the earth and human (*Homo sapiens*) are one of them. Mammals have hair, which is mainly used to maintain the body temperature. In addition to food, which will be discussed later, all mammals need oxygen to generate energy in their bodies. Mammals have certain glands that produce milk. Milk is used by mammalian mothers to feed their babies. Most mammals are born and their fertilization is internal. The brains in mammals are larger than other groups of vertebrates. They usually teach important skills to their offspring. This is very important in development of humans, something which will be discussed later. Although reptiles have teeth but teeth in the mammals have different shapes and are adapted for different types of feeding. Mammals evolved from reptiles about 220 million years ago before evolution of birds. The early form of mammals was probably insect eater. Mammals are divided into three major groups. Of these, the placental mammals are discussed here. This group, including humans, completes their embryonic development within the uterus and in the uterus, they are joined to their mothers by the placenta. Placental mammals originated about 80-100 million years ago and were divided into several groups. One of these groups was the primate, which include monkeys, apes and humans.

The first primates were small mammals. The shoulder joints of primates along with specific structure in their hands (fingers) help them to manipulate food. They have close eyes and usually have single births. Primates nurture their offspring longer than other vertebrates and are mostly active during days in social behaviors. Modern primates were originated from pre-monkeys, which were living in Africa and Southeast Asia. Fossil records show that the early primates (monkeys) evolved about 40 million years ago in Africa and Asia. Apes are divided into four groups in which gorilla and chimpanzees have the biggest brains and are also more adaptable. Contrary to what is believed, humans did not evolve from chimpanzees. Recent studies, especially at the molecular level, showed that both humans and chimpanzees were diverged from a common cat –size ancestor about 35 million years ago. This means that our grand, grand parents are not monkeys, something that some people are very sensitive about. In other words, never in the past there has been a living organism that has been half man and half monkey! The humans were originated as the result of a series of geological changes about 5 million years ago.

The early-fossilized human skull was discovered in 1924 in South Africa and was named *Australopithecus africanus*. Additional findings showed that *Australopithecus* could walk fully erect, had humanlike hands and teeth but a smaller brain. In 1974, in Ethiopia a well-preserved skeleton of another *Australopithecus* was discovered and was named "Lucy". Scientific studies showed that Lucy lived about 3,000,000 years ago and belonged to another species named *Australopithecus afraensis* that has been the ancestor of *Homo,* our genus. *Australopithecus* could walk upright for nearly one million years before development of its brain. Enlargement of the human brain and changes in the hands took place about 2,000,000 years ago at the time which humans started making stone tools. Early humans could also hunt animals and gather fruits. Fossils found in different places showed that the first humans, *Homo erectus,* migrated from Africa to Europe and Asia and were living from 1,600,000 to about 300,000 years ago with brains as large as 1200 cc. This species lived in caves, could build fire, and make stone tools. About 130,000 to 35,000 years ago, Neanderthals that were descendants of Homo erectus were living in Europe and the Middle East. Neanderthals had bigger brains compare to us and were living along with *Homo sapiens* (human). A number of scientists believe that modern humans had evolved in different parts of the world and resulted in multiregional emergence of *Homo sapiens*. The oldest fossils of *Homo sapiens*, which were about 100,000 years old, were found in Africa and Israel. These fossils showed that in some places *Homo sapiens* and Neanderthals were living close to each other. These two human types did not interbreed and finally Neanderthals disappeared and *Homo sapiens* replaced them. A group of scientists think that *Homo sapiens* evolved in one region in Africa and then migrated outside of Africa. Recent studies on mitochondrial DNA support the idea that *Homo sapiens* evolved in Africa.

Overall, anatomical changes, such as bipedalism, change in vertebral column, enlargement of brains, and changes in the hands along with climate changes in Africa, using tools and consuming high-energy food were the major factors influencing human evolution. The first cultural evolution of man started with hunting and food gathering. Humans started to bury their dead and paint in caves around 40,000 years ago. Development of agriculture took place sometimes around 15,000 years ago and this caused settlements in the cities. General information about the history of humans from 10,000 years ago up to present will be discussed later.

Several scientists suggest that human evolution is complete and no new "human" will evolve anymore. They think technology eliminated natural selection which is the basis of evolution. They also think, in the past strong population destroyed the weak population but at present both strong and weak have access to whatever they want. They even say that poor people have access to food and medicine more than Emperor of China 1000 years ago and there is no need for competition. They also suggest that because of future advancement in technology even dramatic changes in the natural world will have no evolutionary consequences.

I do not agree with the above ideas. I think evolution is a part of nature and it will be continued. If we consider Chinese, Persians, Egyptians, Inca and Indians the oldest civilizations on earth, they are only about 5,000 years old. Evolution is a very slow process and even 50,000 years is nothing for an evolutionary process. I think we are in a phase of "hidden evolution". After all, someone should ask, does everybody really have access to food and medicine? Actually, natural selection starts with struggle for existence. Do not you think that humans are in struggle with each other at any given time? Never in the history of mankind have we had so many problems, like we are having now. I hope my statement does not confuse readers. Struggles between humans does not mean that a new species will be born due to the wars; although, struggles may at last reduce or even eliminate certain population. We will discuss this subject later.

In summary, in this chapter we discussed about the origin of animals and human evolution. We now know that changes, which can be transferred to offspring and produce new population, along with struggle for existence followed by natural selection, are the main processes of evolution. We also learned that humans were not evolved from monkeys, and humans are not different from other forms of life in the evolutionary process. I think evolution is a proved fact in biology. It is worth to mention that in 1999, the Kansas Board of Education voted to remove the subject of evolution and Big Bang from state science curriculum. I wonder how a group of people, in the United States in 1999 reached this decision.

CHAPTER SIX

Animal and Human Behaviors

Study on animal behavior is one of the oldest aspects of biology. Thousands of years ago, learning about animal behavior was essential for human survival. By learning about animal behavior, early humans increased their chances for secure food and survival. A simple definition for behavior is: to act, react, or function to stimulus. Much of behavior is observable due to muscular activities. For example, making sounds by infants is a behavior action that influences their learning ability. The science of behavior in humans, which deal with the subject of human actions, usually includes sociology, social and cultural anthropology, psychology, and behavioral aspects of biology, economics, geography, law, psychiatry, and political science.

By using animal behavior as principal research for human behavior, scientists showed that when dealing with certain behavior usually two types of questions, *why* and *how,* should be answered. When we ask *why* an animal has a certain behavior, we ask about ultimate causation or the reason for existence of something. In contrast, if we ask about *how* an animal carries out a certain behavior, we want to know the mechanisms of the behavior. The *how* and *why* questions about animal behaviors are related to their evolutions. Although genes exert a strong influence on behavior, environment is also a major factor influencing behavior of animals and humans. Study on behavior of animals and humans were originated in 1930 when ethnologists tried to find the reasons for animal behavior in their habitats. One major finding showed that animals carry out many behaviors even without ever seeing them before. In other words, certain behaviors are already programmed in animals and they do them because they are beneficial. In other words, certain behaviors such as interaction of parents with their children are associated with fixed –action patterns. For example, in many bird species when the parent returns to the nest, the blind newly hatched young acts a begging behavior and open its month. In fact, the parent landing on the nest causes behavior of the young. In humans an infant's smile is a fixed –action pattern.

Learning which can be also defined as the modification of behavior experiences is a major factor that is associated with behavior. In fact, learning means acquiring knowledge or developing the ability to perform new behaviors. When we talk about learning, one may say learning is something that takes place in schools, but much of human learning occur at home during childhood and continue throughout our lives in our societies. It is believed that what a child learns up to age seven is equal to what he/she learns during the rest of his/her life. Children learn to walk, to talk, and to use their hands. They use their senses to learn about the sights, sounds, tastes, and smells. They learn how to interact with their parents and other people important to their world. When they enter school, children learn reading, writing, and mathematics. From the surrounding environment they learn which behaviors are likely to be rewarded and which ones are likely to be punished. By interacting with other children and during their adulthood, they learn how to adapt to the many major changes in their lives. They learn about sex, marriage, raising children, and working. This is a period of life which children thinks about religion, being poor, being rich, and get interested in politics and similar subjects. Obviously, the societies have direct influences on our learning.

For example, in a society, in which a certain religion is dominant and there are many restrictions, an adult absorbs to the same religion. Later we will discuss this issue in more detail. Learning continues throughout our lives and affects us on almost everything we do in our lives. At present, nearly all biologists agree that our behavior is the consequence of genetic and environment influences. Since learning is very important, parents and teachers have to understand the correct answers to the questions and try to educate the children in the best and effective ways. Overall, those who deal with human behavior such as psychologists, social workers, and criminologists need to understand how certain experiences change people's behaviors. They should search the children's childhood. A person who does something horrible may have a bad experience in his/her childhood. Maybe he/she has been abused and is therefore trying to seek revenge. Knowing about the learning ability of humans is very important for certain opportunists in the society. Employers, politicians, religious leaders, and advertisers make use of learning capacities and influence on the behavior of people. Learning is related to memory and it is associated with the brain; therefore, we should know how behavior of a person may change because of experiences. Overall, learning can be simple or complex.

Simple learning is associated with effect of a single stimulus. A *stimulus* is something that affects the senses. Light, sound, smell, touch, and taste are stimulus. In this type of learning, a person learns because of stimuli that occur in sequence. In another type of learning, which is called operant conditioning, a person learns by forming an association between a behavior and its consequences. For example, by doing something either gets a reward or it is punished. Humans similar to animals can also learn by observing other humans or animals' behaviors.

Complex forms of learning involve more complicated skills such as learning a language, or analyzing concepts. Learning can be due to habituation, for example, a person's attention is captured by a sudden loud noise. Habituation is very useful because our environments are always full of stimuli and we gradually learn how to respond to them. Habituation is associated with the nervous system and occurs both in humans and animals. Sensitization is another form of learning, which occurs following effect of an intense stimulus. For example, a person who exercised the effect of fire will afterward withdraw his/her hand, which is close to fire faster. Another type of learning is called classical conditioning. In classical conditioning type of learning, a reflexive or response transfers from one stimulus to another one. This type of learning is also called associative learning. This type of learning can be better explained by the work of I. Povlov. In 1900 Povlov sprayed powdered meat into the dogs' mouths causing them to salivate. In his experiments, just before spraying, he exposed the dogs to the sound of a ringing bell. Eventually, he showed that dogs salivated only to the sound of bell alone without any meat. It is believed that associative learning occurs when a person forms a mental association between two stimuli. Humans form these sorts of mental associations between stimuli when they occur close together. Pavlov spent three decades studying the processes of classical conditioning. He could identify four main processes associated with classical conditioning. These processes are acquisition, extinction, generalization, and discrimination.

Explaining the details of these processes are out of the limits of this book; however, we can only briefly discuss the effect of classical conditioning on human behavior. Psychologists tried to find out how classical conditioning can be applied to human behavior. In an experiment performed by J. B. Watson and his associate R. Rayner in 1921, they conditioned a baby to fear a small white rat by pairing the sight of the rat with a loud noise. During this experiment they showed that humans could learn fear due to unimportant stimuli when the stimuli are associated with unpleasant experiences. Their experiment also suggested that classical conditioning could also be associated with some cases of phobias. It is now known that classical conditioning explains many emotional responses including happiness, excitement, anger, and anxiety. Recent works showed that conditioning does not always require a close pairing of the two stimuli. For example, people can stop eating a specific food if they become sick after eating it, even if the sickness begins several hours after eating.

Another type of learning is operant conditioning (also called trail-and error), which involves increasing or decreasing a behavior by following it with a reward or with a punishment. A good example for this type of learning is a reward that a child may receive after doing a certain useful action. In this case, the child's behavior, which is associated with a useful action, increases because of the reward. Most of the early scientific research on operant conditioning has been conducted on rats, cats, dogs, and chickens; however, they can also be applied to humans. Operant conditioning is very important in human behavior. It explains how people learn new behaviors or change existing behaviors for a reward. Conditioning techniques have many applications in ordinary life of humans. For example, parents, teachers, religious leaders, and politicians, can reinforce people to conduct certain behaviors for certain reward. As an example, we can mention the action of the individuals who crashed planes into the World Trading Center in the New York City. They did this action because they were promised to get a reward and go to heaven after they were dead.

Some forms of learning behaviors are related to maturation of humans. Other forms may be due to imprinting certain innate behavior. A good example for imprinting is the young ducks or geese, which follow their mother. The reason which birds follow their mother is not because she is their mother. The young birds do not have any sense for "mother" therefore, when they are young, they may follow what is moving. The moving object can be a human. We can see this type of behavior in humans too. People may show certain behavior without fully understanding the reason.

It is shown that humans can monitor the behavior of other humans and then learn a certain behavior. This type of learning behavior is called observational behavior. Observational learning differs from classical and operant conditioning because it does not require direct experience with stimuli. Learning by observation involves watching the behavior of another person, which is called a *model*. By observational learning an individual will imitate the model's behavior. Humans learn many things through observation, imitating parents, other family members, and friends. Many kinds of animals such as birds, cats, dogs, rodents, and primates can also learn by observing other members of their species. Learning through observation and then imitating a behavior need attention, retention, reproduction, and motivation. The subject of observational learning is a very important part of human behavior and we cannot discuss it in detail. We will explain only those parts which are related to this book. One of the most powerful tools which extensively effect on observational learning is television. In modern societies, television provides many powerful models for human observational learning. Many people are concerned about the behaviors of humans after watching TV. A significant number of television programs include depictions of sex, violence, drug and alcohol use, and bad language. In the past TVs were mostly local and if a bad program was presented on TV, only a small number of people could see it. These days with the help of satellites a program produced in the United States can reach everywhere around the world or vice versa. Example, most Middle East countries have lots of cultural restrictions regarding relations between males and females. In some countries, like Afghanistan under Taliban, these types of restriction were so advanced that women were covered in a way that they could hardly even breathe. The same people could watch TV programs through satellites and see the relation between males and females in the United States. It is clear that the consequence of this type of learning is not good. This subject will be discussed in more detail in the following pages. It is proved that watching violence on television has negative effects on children and increases aggression in them. Obviously, the effects of television on human behavior are not always negative. Educational programs can add to the knowledge of humans.

Learning can also be obtained through other forms of behaviors. Examples are: language learning, learning by listening and reading, concept formation, and the learning of motor skills. There are several factors, which influence the learning ability of individuals. Of these factors four important ones are the individual's *age, motivation, prior experience,* and *intelligence.* Animals and humans of all ages are able to learn by habituation, classical conditioning, and operant conditioning. In Humans from birth to about 2 years of age infants use their senses to learn about their bodies and objects around them. In about 2 to 7 years of age they think about objects and events, which do not exist. From about 7 to 11 years of age children learn general rules about the physical world. In operational stage (ages 11 and up) humans have the ability for logical thinking. Learning is usually most efficient if the learner is motivated. If a person's motivation for learning a subject is too low, a child may give up soon. A very high level of motivation also is not good because it may cause stress.

Learning ability is associated with prior experience. The level of intelligence in humans affects their ability to learn and understand. It is important to mention that a number of disorders may interfere with a person's ability to learn and this has a direct effect on person's behaviors. It should also be noted that animals and humans have behavioral rhythms meaning that they usually do all kinds of repeated behaviors. For example, sleeping at night is a repeated behavior. Also, movement and foraging is a sort of behavior in animal and humans.

Social behavior is another aspect of human behavior. Members of different species usually live close to each other and therefore they are always in interaction. Since individuals in a population have a common niche, there is always a potential for conflict. Sometimes conflict is between members of two populations, which are close to each other. Sometimes the social behavior is antagonistic. In this type of behavior, the reasons for competition between populations are access to resources, such as food or especially in animals for mates. Sometimes the conflict is territorial. In this form of behavior, a population defends its territory and usually excludes the members of another population from their own species. Later we will see that humans behave similar to animals and in fact wars and constant fighting between countries are related to basic aspects of human (animal) behavior.

One of the major differences between plants and animals is the ability of animals to coordinate the activities of their specialized body parts. The activities are coordinated because of internal communication between the *nervous system* and *endocrine system*. The nervous system in animals (humans) conveys high- speed signals along its cells and these signal or messages function in activities such as movements. The coordination in animals is also associated with chemical signals. The hormones of the endocrine system convey information between organs of the body and directly affect body functions. The normal coordination and interaction between these two systems control the physiology and behavior. For example, the signals from these systems actually cause fight or fights responses in animals.

In humans, one of the most important classes of social behavior is verbal behavior. Humans' cultural evolution took place because humans can listen, write, read and talk. In fact these abilities are the main difference between humans and animals. We can see the basic function of verbal communication when someone talks to one or a group of people. When humans talk, they expect their speech to induce listeners to engage in some sort of behavior. Obviously, if the main reason for a speech is something positive, it will be useful for the listeners. In contrast, if a person who is giving the talk has a negative attitude, the listeners may get engaged in unpleasant behavior.

In this chapter, up to this point, we briefly discussed the role of genetic and environment in our ability to learn. We also noted that human behaviors are directly related to their ability to learn and age, society and other environmental factors are very important in our learning abilities. We also know by now that for a normal behavioral function, the physiology of our bodies, especially nervous and endocrine systems should function properly. This means that in humans, a combination of many factors results in our behaviors. Obviously, a healthy individual, with a good learning capacity, and normal childhood can behave normal and be productive in society. In contrast, a person whose life has been associated with different abnormal issues is not considered normal. Since different humans have different childhood, social, economic, cultural, learning ability and experiences, they have different personalities and behave in different ways. In other words, in any society there are several people who have some sort of mental disorder. Discussing about mental disorders is out of the limit of this book. Overall, there are over 60 different types of well-known mental disorders. Here we only generally discuss mental illness and especially emphasize on the crime.

Mental disorders are generally characterized by disturbances in persons' thoughts, emotions, or behavior. The term *mental illness* refers to a wide variety of disorders, ranging from those that cause mild distress to those that severely impair a person's ability to function. Mental health professionals sometimes use the terms *psychiatric disorder* for patients who suffer from a mental disorder. It is very important to know that not all individuals with mental problems show the symptoms of their illnesses. For example, a person who can easily kill another person may absolutely look normal to others in his/her ordinary life. The symptoms of a number of mental illnesses can be very distressing. For example, persons with schizophrenia may hear voices inside their head that command them to act in strange or unpredictable ways.

Experiences of mental illness often differ depending on people's culture and social backgrounds. In most societies mental illness carries substantial shame. The mentally ill are often blamed.

Ordinary people may see mentally ill individuals as victims of bad fate, religious and moral transgression. In each society a significant number of people have some sort of mild or sever cases of mental problem. For example, in the world, about 500 million people suffer from depression. In the United States, 20 percent of people can expect to get some form of depression in their lifetime. Economic cost of mental illness is relatively high. To give you an idea, in 1985 the economic costs of mental illness in the United States totaled $103.7 billion. In the world a universally accepted definition for mental illness does not exist and a definition of mental illness depends on a society's norms. Because norms vary between cultures, behaviors considered signs of mental illness in one culture might be considered normal in other cultures.

It is obvious that some sort mental disorders may end in committing a crime. Crime is commission of an act that violates the law. The law may be local or universal. For example, there are societies in which homosexuality is a crime and is punishable. In contrast, there are societies in which homosexuality is free and even two homosexuals can officially marry. The punishment for a crime is also not the same all over the world even in one community. For example, in society a person may be executed for stealing but in the same society, the leader of the same society may kill thousands of people with chemicals and still be considered the leader of the society.

In most countries, crimes are punishable. Punishments may include death, imprisonment, exile, fines, and removal from the job. The problem, which is facing humans, is the fact that sometimes those who write the punishment laws are immune to their own law. For example, a person or a group of people may kill thousands of people by the most disgusting methods only because they have different religion or belong to another race. Interestingly, the same person or group may be considered a hero in the same society. Severe cases of mental illnesses almost always alter people life and usually a sick person cannot hold a job. As noted above, unfortunately, in some cases of mental disorders the sick person does not manifest any symptoms.

For thousands of years humans tried to understand the causes of mental disorders. Biologists consider mental disorders as changes in the body process and psychologists emphasize on the roles of a person's upbringing and environment. Emil Kraepelin believed that psychiatric disorders were diseases similar to physical illnesses. On the other hand, S. Freud argued that the source of mental illness lay in unconscious conflicts originating in early childhood experiences. Today, it is believed that a combination of both biology and a person's environment play important roles in mental illness. For example, an infant may inherit genes that could enable him/her to become a tall person, but this may not happen due to malnourished. Likewise, an individual who does not possess a biological vulnerability for depression may never become severely depressed.

Finally, every person has specific characteristics, such as thinking, feeling, behaving, and relating to others. The specific characteristics of each person are referred to as personality. Most people experience at least some difficulties that result from their personality and therefore they have personality disorders. People with personality disorders usually justify their motivations and relate their actions to cultural behavior. Many personality disorders represent extreme variants of behavior patterns. A behavior that seems unusual to one person may look normal to another depending on gender, ethnicity, and cultural background. About 20 percent of people in the general population have some sort of personality disorders. Of these, a significant number of them have other mental illnesses.

In summary, in this chapter we briefly discussed human and animal behaviors. We now know that although our genes have influence on our behaviors, environment is also a major influencing factor. Environment factors can be our parents, teachers, or leaders. A number of humans' behaviors are cultural; therefore, it may have different meaning in various societies. We know that our behaviors are heavily associated with our learning ability. In some instances, humans act like animals and have different sorts of behaviors, such as defending territory. Finally, a significant number of people who look normal may have some sort of mental disorder. The problem which humans are facing now is the fact that sometimes a mentally ill person becomes a raw model and ordinary people in a society may follow the model. We will get back to this subject in the following chapters.

CHAPTER SEVEN

Human Nutrition

Generally, humans are advanced animals and therefore similar to animals are always searching for food. In other words, the first and the most important need of all animals, including human is food and eating is a behavior. As discussed before, green plants and green algae are the main provider of food on earth. Plants produce organic components in their cells during the photosynthesis process and use them for their own metabolisms. Herbivores animals eat dead or fresh plants and carnivores consume plant- eater animals. Omnivores, such as humans, consume both animal and plant material. It is believed that consuming diets rich in animal material had an evolutionary effect on the size of human brains in the past.

For a healthy life, all organisms need certain organic and inorganic compounds that are generally named "essential nutrients". The food used by all animals, including humans, is used for biosynthesis and as energy (calorie) source. For essential nutrients all animals depend on plants and their needs vary from species to species. It is interesting to mentions that something, which can be a good source of food for an organism, may not be essential for another organism. Humans take nearly all their needs from other organisms. If in the diet of a person one or more essential nutrient is missing this individual is malnourished. Malnutrition is common in human populations and we are all witness of food deficiencies in most part of the world. In addition to water, which is the most important chemical for life, there are five other classes of essential nutrients. These nutrients are proteins (amino acids), fat (fatty acids), carbohydrates, vitamins and minerals. Of these, proteins are very important because they are essential for muscles, bones, antibodies production, and enzymes. Different animals obtain these nutrients by various methods including competition and interactions between each other. Of different types of interactions, one, which is mostly seen in the wild animals, is a condition by which an organism (predator) eats another organism (pray). In another type of interaction between animals, which is named symbiotic interactions, two partners have food relation. In symbiotic interaction two species live close to each other and usually have balanced food relations. Sometimes the relation between two partners is in a way which one organism (the parasite) harms the other one (host). This type of relation is called parasitism. In parasitism, both organisms are alive but there is a possibility that the host die because of massive parasite actions. Sometimes one-partner benefits without significant effect on the other partner. This type of relation is called commensalisms. In the third type of interaction, which is called mutualism, both partners benefit from a relationship. Humans are the only species, which obtain their food by all different types of interactions between species. During their evolutionary process, humans gradually learned specific methods to increase the number of those organisms that could be their food source. This process, which is generally called "agriculture", will be discussed in more detail in this chapter.

Different animals, including humans, usually live very close to their food sources and form communities. In a community there are always different types of completions between all members of the community. Although the geographic distributions of most species are determined by their adaptations and environmental factors, humans usually do not follow geographic patterns and can settle in different geographic parts of the earth. The main factors influencing the settlement of communities are desired temperature, good soil, and water source (enough rainfall). This is clearly seen in the early and recent human communities. Most early human communities have started in places, which had desired temperature, good soil and rivers, e.g. early Egyptian and Middle East countries. It is obvious that early settlements of human caused tense competition between human and human and other species and human. Formation of large cities has been the result of gradual replacement of human population by weaker competitors. Increase in the number of individuals in the early human communities resulted in more food consumption and therefore search for additional food source. The apparent need for food in human communities-initiated agriculture. As a result, communities, which could best improve vegetation and agriculture in their communities, had a better chance of survival. Gradual increases in the human population also created human disturbances due to daily activities.

For example, logging and clearing farmland for agriculture gradually have reduced the forests size all around human communities. Early communities were very small and therefore they were very close to their lands. With increase in the population size in the cities, humans faced transport issues and food distribution issues. Early humans were hunter and were hunting animals for food. In more civilized human communities, gradually animals were adapted for hard work both in agriculture and transportation. The use of

87

mechanical and then machinery agriculture were the results of improvement in human ingenuity. Discovery of coal and later oil is possibly one of the most important achievements of humans.

Both coal and oils are fossils of organisms, which were living on the earth million years ago. Many individuals have considered the use of coal and oils as energy sources in agriculture and transportation as the most important factors in development of industrial society. At present production of food and its transport from one place to another is highly dependent on fossil energy. Of these energy sources, oil is the major factor in every human ordinary life. Although oil is used in petrochemical industry and for temperature-controlled environment, its use in agriculture and transportation is so important that we should consider it as important as food itself. We will discuss this subject in the following chapters.

If we review human history, we will see that early humans were always at war for territory, food, and sexual mates. With gradual improvements in mankind, ideological beliefs also became a reason for wars between human populations. Not very long ago, another major factor, i.e. energy source, was added to human needs and this factor by itself, now became the major cause of tensions between different communities. Obviously, communities, which were settled in better environments, had better lands, and more food sources tried to create borders for their communities. This is considered as the onset of a "country" formation. The discovery of oil in certain parts of the world made a number of countries more valuable than others and therefore tensions were escalated. We will discuss this important economic issue in the following pages. Here we only emphasize on the fact that food is the major need for existence of humans and food production is highly dependent on a relatively cheap energy source. Since plants and a number of domestic animals are the main source of food for humans, we will briefly review agricultural factors, which influence better production of foods. The food security in the world will also be discussed.

Even before humans began to develop agriculture (about 10,000 years ago), early humans everywhere have discovered the food value of plants and animals. Agriculture is the art, science, and industry of managing the growth of plants and animals for human use. In other words, agriculture includes cultivation of the soil, growing and harvesting crops, breeding, dairying, and forestry. Modern and productive agriculture depend on the engineering and technology which are directly associated with energy sources. Mechanization of agriculture started in the late 19th and early 20th centuries and so far, has enormously increased farms' efficiency and productivity. Overall, only a small number of countries fully mechanized their agriculture. A number of undeveloped countries still use animals such as horses and oxen to cultivate their fields, harvest crops, and transport farm products. Agricultural is not necessarily associated with food.

Nonfood crops such as tobacco are also a part of agriculture however it is harmful for humans. At present, nearly 48 percent labor force in the world is in the business of agriculture. The distribution of people who are engaged in the agriculture is not the same all over the world. In the United States about 3 percent of population is engaged in the agriculture and the same 3 percent not only produce food for use in the United States but also export it to other countries. In Africa 60 percent of population are in the business of agriculture and still depend on food from other developed countries. The farm size is a major factor in agriculture. Developed countries have larger farms compared to underdeveloped countries. Much of the foreign exchange earned by a number of countries is derived from

89

agricultural products. This means that trade in agriculture is always an international concern. The Food and Agricultural Organization (FAO) of the United Nations is directly engaged with agricultural issues in the world

The agriculture on the earth started with the early farmers who mainly occupied southwestern Asia, Iran, Iraq, Israel, Jordan, Syria, (Tigris and Euphrates rivers) Turkey, and Egypt. Archeological findings showed that agriculture has also been done in China, India, Pakistan, and Mexico a long time ago. Carbon-14 dating proved that sheep, goats and cattle were domesticated about 10,000 years ago in Iraq and Iran; and goats were domesticated 8000 years ago in central Iran. Carbon-14 dating also showed that wheat and barley were cultivated in the Middle East about 10,000 years ago, rice in China about 8,000 years ago and squash in Mexico about 10,000 years ago. Early farmers were communities living in small homes closed to their farms. Country living has developed later in different parts of Europe and Asia.

The introduction of metals in tools used in the agriculture has a major influence in agriculture. With the help of better tools, many vegetables and fruits were grown about 5000 years ago in the Middle East. Cotton was grown in India and silk were used extensively in China about 4000 years ago. Gradually, storage methods were improved in the Middle East, India, Egypt, Greece, and Rome and people started to trade food and nonfood items. Irrigation systems in China, Egypt, and the Middle East were expanded and more land was used for cultivation.

Use of labor in agriculture was first developed in the state of Sumer (now Iraq) and gradually use of fertilizer in agriculture was increased. Due to Arabs' influences, Middle Eastern agriculture was extended to Egypt and later to Spain and other European countries. In a period of time, in Egypt, grain production of wheat was enough for the country and international markets. In Spain, vineyards were planted and in the Middle East area, oranges, lemons, peaches, and apricots were cultivated. By the 12th century agriculture in the Middle East had declined and invading Mongols destroyed irrigation systems. The Crusades increased European contact with Islamic lands and brought their ideas to Europe. Gradually, in southern Europe olive oil was used instead of butter, leather was produced from cattle and sheep were used for production of wool. Along with the increase in the population in Europe in the 16th century agricultural was expanded. Europe was cut off from Asia and the Middle East by an extension of Ottoman power and a new period of global exploration and colonization started. From the 15—19th century the slave trade provided laborers for agriculture and slaves replaced indigenous people. Slaves from Africa were transferred to cultivate cotton in the southern United States. Native Americans became slaves in Mexico and gradually new forms of agriculture were moved to South America where Aztec, Inca, and Maya already had intensive agricultural economies. The scientific revolution resulting from the Renaissance in Europe affected agriculture as well as other fields and gradually plant and animal breeding were developed. The first scientific farming was initiated in England and from 1660 large landowners had begun to form. By the mid-19th century machinery agriculture was introduced and in the late 1800s, steam power was used to transport agricultural products. Improvement in transportation extensively affected agriculture. Roads, canals, and rail lines enabled farmers to obtain their needs and transfer their products to wider areas. Food could be protected during transport more economically. Following World

War II (1939-1945), due to the population explosion the need for food was increased and new cultivation methods were adapted.

Agriculture in the United States had progressed significantly in the 20th century and American farmers became more innovative using various types of power machinery on the farms. In the 20th century, steam, gasoline, diesel, and electric power came into wide use. The use of chemical fertilizers was greatly increased and soil erosion was extensively combated. Selective breeding improved strains of both farm animals and crop plants. New uses for farm products and agricultural wastes were discovered. Standards of quality, size, and packing were established and freeze-drying and irradiation were applied for many perishable foods. Scientific methods were applied to control the pests. Since the 1970s improvement in technology farming, such as use of hybrids, better methods of soil conservation and irrigation, and use of fertilizers have led to the production of more food. In recent years, biotechnology helped to increase agricultural productivity by producing genetically engineered plant. To keep the farming as an essential part of the U.S. economy, the U.S. government started to support the farmers after World War I (1914-1918), a policy which significantly helped improvement in agriculture in the U.S. Gradually with well-organized policies including rural economy development, agriculture market-promotion programs, and dairy subsidies, the U.S. government provided better opportunities for U.S. farmers. Based on the soil properties, distance to market, climate, storage, and marketing facilities, ten main farming regions in the U.S. were established and each region became the center for production of certain food products.

The history of agriculture in the United States is a good example showing the efficiency of a good program for production of more food. According to the 1990 U.S. census, in the United States about 4.6 million people lived in the farms. These people not only produce the food needed to feed Americans, but also can produce relatively cheap food for a significant number of people in the rest of the world, especially poor countries. Studies showed that with increase in population, in coming years the world food requirements would increase tremendously and therefore the food prices would increase accordingly. This means that in a near future the whole world will face a major food crisis. Overall, at present the United States is the world's major exporter of agricultural products. In 1995 the value of agricultural products exported by US was about $54.1 billion.

At present, obtaining enough food is an important concern for every nation in the world, and in some country's food shortage is an extremely serious problem. Worldwide, about 14 percent (840 million) of the total world population does not have adequate food. These people suffer from nutrient deficiency that causes general weakness and fatal diseases. Producing enough food does not necessarily guarantee that these people who need it are able to get it. Countries, which do not have enough money to buy food or expand their agriculture, try to somehow find the money. Simply, the countries with poor agriculture need foreign exchange to buy their foods from western countries. Obviously, a number of wealthy countries (such as Saudi Arabia) spend a part of their income to import food. On the other hand, countries, which do not have natural resources, try to get what they need by other methods. A good example is Afghanistan. In this country low-cost narcotic materials are produced and are exported to western countries in the exchange for currency to buy food and other things. Bad economic policies and ideological wars, which are constantly in progress in several countries, is a major factor, which prevents progress in these countries. We will discuss these issues later.

A major problem associated with food production in the world is the fact that the number of farmers worldwide has been gradually decreasing in recent years. Farmers, especially in underdeveloped countries, migrated to the cities to find better work and better income. Food production requires water, productive lands and some form of cheap energy. These vital resources are not distributed evenly around the world. Scientists estimated that during the last 60 years more than 17 percent of the earth's vegetated surface have been degraded, or made less productive by human mismanagement. Water, which is an essential need for the growth of all crops, is in the shortest supply. More than 40 countries lack sufficient water to grow enough food for their people. A number of countries in Africa and the Middle East face periodic drought, which contributes to severe food shortages. If current population trend continues, in about 25 years nearly 75 percent of Africans will face real food shortage. Increase in the population is another factor, which has a reverse effect on agriculture. Homes, shopping centers, industries, and roads replace about 8 million acres of farmland each year. Soil erosion and lack of good farming techniques are a major concern in agriculture. Modern farming techniques depend on extensive use of oil for a variety of tasks especially operating machines used in agriculture. In the United States, agriculture consumes about 17 percent of total energy expenditures. Not all countries can afford such fuel consumption. Not to mention that, fossil fuel supplies cannot last forever. They will be finished in a near future. Moreover, extensive use of fossil fuels is already damaging the environment including air, soil, and water pollution. It has also affected ozone depletion. Ozone Layer and global warming will be discussed later.

At present the world's population is about 6.1 billion and it is projected that it will reach 8 billion by the year 2025. Food production must keep up with the same speed as with the increasing number of people living on the planet. It is believed that in the future in most countries' food production may not match population growth. Population growth negatively affects food production and security. For example, countries may not have enough water for agriculture due to the growing population. Uncontrolled population may lead to disasters and famine in the world in coming years. As discussed above, countries that cannot grow or buy enough food are dependent on food aid from wealthier countries. Interestingly the majority of these countries experience natural disaster or political disruption. A variety of historical, religion, social and economic forces prevented many countries to plan food security in their countries. A number of countries in Africa still have European-owned plantations and produce food only for export. They use their income to buy other things from developed countries. Overall, wars, political disruption, and environmental factors damaged agriculture and reduced food production during the past decade in many countries. For example, in the past 20 years, wars and natural disasters caused a series of food related problems in Afghanistan. Nearly all countries in the Middle East region are somehow in trouble.

Although several organizations such as the Consultative Group on International Agricultural Research (CGIAR), the United States Department of Agriculture, the United Nations Food and Agriculture Organization (FAO) and the United Nations Children's Fund (UNICEF) are trying to help hungry people around the world but it seems food supply will be a major factor facing the world in the future.

In this chapter we briefly discussed the importance of food for humans and problems associated with its production. The history of agriculture and problems related to food shortage in the future were discussed. We could easily show that the countries in the Middle

East which were the first communities developing agriculture are now facing food problem or will have problems soon. It seems the simple agricultural methods applied in the Middle East gradually got complicated and transferred to the western parts of the world. Later we will see that this pattern is also happening in other social behaviors. Since the food supply has been a major reason for wars in all societies, one can predict that this problem get will even worse in coming years. One of the main reasons that the United States is a target is the wealth in this country. We will discuss this issue in more details in the following chapters. The possible solution for the food crisis will also be discussed.

CHAPTER EIGHT

History of Human Races

Generally, history talks about all known events, which took place in the past, and the history of humans deal with the written documents kept from these events. Of all the nations in the world, the Chinese possibly wrote the longest and most voluminous records about their past. In old China, the lessons of history were an integral part of all Chinese learning, an attitude strongly emphasized by Confucius. Chinese wrote the history of each dynasty clearly according to the events.

Many Asian people started to write historical events many centuries ago and perhaps the most familiar one is the history of the Jewish traditions. Of the oldest nations in the world, Persians were possibly the first nation who believed in equal freedom of religions. Muslim historical records are mostly influenced by religious belief. Muslim historians especially recorded the lives of political and military leaders of their time and emphasized on spiritual progress of their societies. Islam believes in equality of the people and does not differentiate between individuals of different colors or nations. A Muslim historian, Ibn Khaldun, in the 14th century suggested that historical changes in the societies are associated with social and economic reasons.

Western historiography originated with the work of ancient Greeks. In the 5th century BC, Herodotus, who is considered the father of history, wrote about the Persian Wars and later Thucydides wrote about War between Athens and Sparta. Their writings have been mainly based on testimony of eyewitness reports and evidence. In their writing they mostly discussed the character of the leaders. The Greek and later Roman historians searched into religion, customs, names and arts and recorded their findings. Greek historians explained Roman history and recorded their political life and military successes. Most early Roman history has been recorded in Greek language. Plutarch wrote the most famous Greek and Roman history in his biographies. During the 4th century Christianity became legal and therefore influenced the Roman Empire and introduced new approaches to history. Eusebius of Caesarea traced the growth of the church from its origins and described religious life, books, ideas, and people. St. Augustine explained the complex relations between Christian and secular history. The Jews history, including Jewish religion and customs was the first written by Flavius Josephus.

During the Middle Ages, in the 5th century AD, with the disintegration of the Roman Empire, the historiography was disrupted and gradually Literacy became a skill of the clergy and studies on religious culture were expanded. Monks started to record whatever they knew of the events. From the 16th century onward, many historians in Europe collected the sources of religious documents. Many modern historians traced the intellectual foundations of historical writing in the 19th-century Germany.

Most of the early historical documents recorded the wars between nations and especially emphasized on the heroes of the wars. In this book, attempts have been made to analyze the reasons for wars between populations, especially in the last century. Many factors contributed to the conflicts between humans. Of these factors, several of them including, fighting for territory, food resources, religions, energy, and races are the most important ones. In this chapter we only discuss about the history of race in human conflicts.

The term, race, has been used to describe a human population distinguishable from others based on shared biological traits. As we already know, all humans belong to one species named *Homo sapiens*. In other words, we cannot exactly separate humans into defined races. Most scientists do not believe in biological race and instead see humans as biological variations. In spite of many scientific supporting facts, today the subject of human race is a powerful social and cultural problem that divides people into the races based on their physical appearance and behaviors. Around the world, human populations differ in their skin color, eye color and shape, hair color and texture, body shape, and other physical characteristics. It is believed that differences between populations is largely superficial, resulting from adaptations to local environment during the recent period of human evolution. Genetic analysis, reveals that overall, people are remarkably similar in their genetic makeup. Today, most anthropologists reject the idea that "pure" races existed at some time in the distant past. The term *race* is often misunderstood and is confused with *ethnicity*, something that is mostly related to cultural differences between groups. Ethnic groups derive their identities from their distinctive customs, languages, ancestry, places of origin, or style of their dresses. People also misuse the term *"race"* to refer to a religion, culture, or nationality, such as the "Jewish race" or the "Italian race". Many people falsely believe that differences in the physical appearance are related to differences in the behavior, attitude, and intelligence of people. These beliefs promote *racism*, prejudice or animosity against people perceived to belong to other races. This is why racism has inspired the abuse and extermination of enormous numbers of people in the past and unfortunately in the present. The best examples for racism are the use of Africans by European settlers in the America as slaves in the 16th-20th century, the extermination of Jews in Europe by German Nazis during World War II (1939-1945); or apartheid in South Africa. Overall, genetic analysis proved that on the surface of the earth we do not have different races of humans. As discussed before, studies suggest that all humans are descended from a relatively small group of humans who lived in eastern Africa and then migrated out of Africa about 50,000 years ago.

To examine the concept of human races we should briefly discuss about the origin of races. Since ancient times, explorers traveled to foreign lands and wrote about the differences among human populations around the world. The history of racism possibly starts from the 2nd century when Roman Empire reached its height territories in the Middle East, North Africa, and Eastern Europe. The Romans started trading goods with India, while China established the Silk Road. The Silk Road ran from China to India, the Middle East, and Roman ports on the Mediterranean Sea. These trade routes established links among people and cultures. During the age of European exploration in the 15th and 16th centuries, several western European countries including Portugal, Spain, The Netherlands, England, and France started to explore regions of the world that were largely unknown to Europeans. Rulers and leaders of these countries paid for these voyages with the hopes of controlling the foreign lands for their economic and political benefit. The explorers gradually came to believe that different customs were somehow directly related to differences in the skin color, hair color and texture, and body and face shape. Therefore, they used the term *race* to describe the physical and cultural differences among people.

In the 1200s Europeans did not know much about East Asia. They could not believe the reports of explorer Marco Polo who traveled to China and countries of Southeast Asia. Polo described the highly populated China and unfamiliar customs there. He wrote about having paper money for trade, using coal and oil for fuel, and printing ability. Although Polo recorded the skin color and appearance of the people in China, he did not mention the term race in his writings. In the 15th century, contact between Europe and America began with the voyages of Italian-Spanish navigator Christopher Columbus.

In his writing Columbus wrote about people of the islands of the Caribbean. He recorded details of their skin, black hair, and short muscular bodies. He mentioned about their habits of going largely unclothed and bathing frequently. Soon the Spaniards began to clash over Native Americans and killed a great number of indigenous people, a pattern that was followed for centuries by Spanish, Portuguese, French, and British colonists of the Americas.

In the1700s, James Cook from Britain, traveled to the South Pacific and in contrast to what other European explorers did in the region, he treated the people in the area with respect. The British settled in Australia in the late 1700s and early 1800s. The British settlers of Australia soon met the Aboriginal hunters and regarded them as an inferior race. Clashes of white settlement in Australia led to massive Aboriginal deaths enslavement and displacement of native Australians.

Contemporary with European explorations, a Swedish botanist and physician named Carolus Linnaeus in the mid-1700s wrote that humans are related to monkeys and apes. Later Linnaeus subdivided humans into four main subspecies; however he did not refer to them as races. He named these races as, people of the Americas; people of European, people of Asian; and people of African. Later the classification studies of Linnaeus were used by others to associate different temperaments and cultural traits with each subspecies. During the 18th century, Christian scholars suggested the Great Chain of Being. They assumed that God is in the top and below God were living things, with humans at the top and other animals ranked lower. Although Linnaeus did not exactly rank humans, his subspecies classification implied ranking of Europeans first, followed by Asians and Americans, with Africans at the bottom. French naturalist George-Louis Leclerc, Comte de Buffon, described the human diversity in a different way and rejected racial classification. Instead, he described the variety of behaviors among human populations; however, in 1749 he was the first person who used the term *race* to refer to a local population. He believed that all people belonged to one biological group and differences in human populations resulted directly from environmental conditions. In the late 1700s German physician Johann Blumenbach proposed another racial classification system. He divided humans into five races or varieties: Caucasian, Mongolian, Malayan, Ethiopian, and American. Later, Blumenbach's classification was described as the white, yellow, brown, black, and red races. Despite all these classifications, all scientists of the time believed that humans were different from all other animals. Blumenbach used the term *Caucasian* to describe the race of white European people. Blumenbach's classification finally ended to a conclusion that Caucasians are superior to other races. In the 1830s Belgian statistician, Adolphe Quételet, suggested a theory based on statistical findings. Later scientists tried to establish and confirm the racial categories based on anatomical features. During the 19th century scientists became interested in *anthropometry* and used the head shape and size to divide people. Samuel G. Morton in the 1830s and 1840s conducted several studies on more than 1,000 skulls and concluded that human races did not share a common ancestor. After Morton's death in 1851, a number of his followers used his work to justify the slavery arguing that blacks were different from whites. As we now know, in the 1850s British naturalist Charles Darwin developed the theory of natural selection and biological evolution. Darwin thought that human variations are not related to taxonomic organization; however, supporter of different races rejected Darwin's theory and still believed that races were fixed.

During the 20th century, scientists continued to understand human diversity. In 1942, when Nazi Germany was using the racial superiority to justify the killings of millions of Jews, Ashley Montagu discussed about race as *Man's Most Dangerous Myth*. In 1950 biologists and anthropologists met and argue about the human origins, evolution, and race and reached to the conclusion that race was only a classificatory convenience and not a physical reality. During 1950 to 1970s the United Nations Educational, Scientific, and Cultural Organization (UNESCO) published a series of statements on race. In these statements, UNESCO declared a goal for eliminating racism around the world.

Today, the human variation at the genetic level provides convincing evidence that refutes the human races. As discussed in chapter five, today the scientific data strongly support the idea that humans originated not a long time ago from a relatively small population and all of them share a strong genetic heritage. In other words, they are much more alike than different. The differences among people are mostly noticeable in the skin color, body shape, facial features, and hair color and texture. Many of these differences evolved due to adaptations to the environments in which our ancestors lived. Although the biological concept of race is rejected in many societies the idea suggesting that people belong to different races is still a major problem. Some people still believe that they belong to a particular race and therefore they consider themselves in a different social category. In several societies these groups influence their governments and their actions finally cause discrimination and conflict between individual in a population or in two populations. At present, the concept of race and cultural differences, such as language or religion became important political issues in the countries and caused wars between diverse populations. Much of human suffering throughout history has resulted directly from racism and racial discrimination. Examples are slavery in the Americas or superiority of Aryan race believed by the Nazi Party of Germany, which resulted in the horrific holocaust, against Jews. Sometimes the mistreatment of a certain group of people is based on *ethnic conflict* or cultural differences. Examples for ethnic conflict are the wars among Serbian, Croatian, Bosnian Muslim, and Albanian ethnic groups in the former Yugoslavia during the 1990s.

In summary, in spite of much supporting scientific data, which reject the concept of race in humans and emphasize on similarity between them, there are still individuals who believe in the superiority of certain races. Unfortunately, a number of these individuals have enough political power to create conflicts around the world. Using race as a reason for killing innocent people should be absolutely rejected and whatever humans did in the past to justify racism are only dark points in the history of mankind.

CHAPTER NINE

Human Population

Human population refers to a total number of individuals who inhabit a specific area, such as a city, country, or continent, at a given time. Demography means study on the population and it deals with the size, composition, and distribution of the population. It also means study on changes in population patterns including births, deaths, and migration. In Biology, population refers to the study of animals and plants, which can interbreed in a specific region. A given population is usually isolated and its variability, density, and stability, are affected by several factors. These factors include, birth and death rates, ages and sex, behavioral patterns, relationships with other species, food supplies, migration patterns and availability of space for expansion. One of the most important characteristics of a population is its tendency to disperse from a region where the density of their numbers is high to a region with a lower density. This is good for those, which move to a new territory where their chance for food resources may increase. The history of demography started with the theory of British economist, Thomas Robert Malthus (1766-1834), in 1798. According to Malthus theory, population size usually increases faster than the supply of food available for its need; therefore, the population growth became controlled by famine, disease, and war. The conclusion of Malthus theory states that population should somehow be controlled.

For example, in the 1950 the world population was 2.5 billion and it is estimated to be 9 billion in 2050.

As discussed above factors such as births, deaths, immigrants, and emigrants determine the population sizes. These factors by themselves are under control by other factors. For example, a healthy population with a relatively large number of old people may have a similar death rate compared to a poor population composed of younger members. In these two populations, however the death rates are the same but the second population may disappear over the time. This means that life expectancy in a population is one major factor affecting a population size. Another example is the rate of birth compared to the rate of death. In some parts of the world the birth rate compared to death rate is high and therefore in these places the population size increases faster than other populations, which have lower birth rates. Infant mortality rate, which is highly associated with the public health, is also a major factor affecting the population size. The overall public health in any population is directly related to the economy and availability of food in the same population. Another major factor affecting the population size is religious belief. Some people do not participate in family planning programs because of their religious belief about life.

According to the United Nation estimates, the world population was about 300 million in the year 1 AD. It reached to 600 million in 1,600. Starting in the 17th century, better agriculture, industry, medicine, and social organization caused rapid increase in the population growth. In 1900 the world population reached 1.65 billion, and by 1960 it was 3.02 billion. It is estimated that the world population will reach to 9 billion in 2050 as a result of better medicine, improved agriculture, better public health, and improvement in water supplies. Later we will see that improvement in all aspects of life cannot provide essential support for the needs of human population in the future and we need to look for solutions to control human population. Gradual development in many third world countries caused major changes from agricultural to an industrial economy; therefore, large numbers of rural residents migrated to towns and cities in these countries. These migrations had two major effects in developed countries. One major issue is related to low productivity of agricultural products, which means dependency on foreign food supply; and the second issue was creation of over populated cities and towns. Obviously, rich countries, especially in the Middle East (example Iran) could afford to buy foreign food to feed their over populated cities. In contrast, poor countries (example Afghanistan) faced social and economic problems. Later we will discuss the form of governments in this region of the world and discuss unemployment in this area. We will also see why young people in these societies, joined religious movements, and created a new chapter in the history of mankind on earth.

In spite of the family planning programs in most countries in the world, it is estimated that the world population will gradually increase. At present, in developed nations the issue of a national population policy is serious and governments address plans for population growth control. Unfortunately, in most third world countries, especially in Africa, the uncontrolled growth of population is either not seriously considered or it is only partially in place. In 1952, India which is the second most populated nation in the world, adopted a policy to slow its population growth and a significant number of people participated in the efficient contraception and family-planning programs. China, which is the most populated nation in the world, also lowered the population growth in its nation by an efficient population policy and could successfully reduce both fertility and mortality. At present, about ninety percent of the world's births and seventy seven percent of world's deaths occur in the third world countries.

In coming years, regional and global population changes will be influenced by several factors, such as:

1. Differences in the rate of fertility and the rate of mortality.
2. The uncertain future growth rates in the highly populated countries
3. Family planning services.
4. The course of the AIDS pandemic, especially in Africa.

Generally, at present, each year increase in the world population is equivalent to adding the population of a new Israel, Egypt, Jordan, West Bank, and Gaza to the world.

Of the most important factors affecting the population sizes are immigration and emigration. The movement of people from one nation into another nation or region with the intention of permanent residency is called immigration. The term emigration refers to the movement of people from their leaving nation. Immigration is a worldwide phenomenon and is a serious issue for several countries in the world. Starting in the17th century up to 19th century, millions of Europeans migrated to North America, South America, some parts of Africa and Australia. Immigrants resettled in other countries in search of jobs and business opportunities. Today, most immigrants who move to developed countries are from less developed and poorer countries. A significant number of these immigrants leave their own nations because of many political, religious and economic reasons and overall are considered refugees. Wars, corrupted governments, and natural disasters are the main reasons, which force refugees to leave their homeland. After World War I and World War II, most refugees were from eastern European countries. In recent years most refugees are from the Middle East countries and Africa. A number of these refugees are searching for political asylum and therefore look for prosperous and democratic countries. One of the most important issues regarding these refugees is the fact that a significant number of them are the most educated people in their own nations. This means that a number of these countries not only cannot advance the general knowledge of their own nations but also simply loose the existing educated people too. This is one of the most important factors, which created recent problems in the world. For immigrants and refugees, the best part and the most democratic place in the world is the United States.

Since its establishment, America has always absorbed immigrants as laborers and new settlers. The majority of immigrants moved to the United States for jobs and to search for better life. A small number of immigrants who moved to the United States left their countries because of political or religious reasons. Regardless of the reasons for immigration of people to the United States, this country, which is the most advanced nation in the world, is built by immigrants. Immigrants from certain nations try to keep their own cultural heritage, language, and religious practices. In other words, a significant number of immigrants continue to value their heritage and therefore sometimes directly or indirectly try to help their own people too. Nevertheless, today, most America's immigrants are proud of being Americans.

As discussed, population aging and the life expectancy are other factors affecting population size. In different nations aging is not the same. For example, a baby born in Sub-Saharan Africa is more likely to die in infancy compared to a child born in a developing region. At present the life expectancy in Western Europe is 78 years and in Sub-Saharan Africa is 49 years.

No matter what factor causes the increase in the population of a region, the result is the fact that a populated region needs food and other services. Most people in poor countries need housing, effluent disposal, roads, transportation, and other infrastructure basic of government services. At least 220 million urban people lack access to clean drinking water; more than 420 million do not have access to other bare essentials of living. Despite the significant progress in almost all developing countries, more than 1.3 billion people in the developing world still struggle to survive on less than a dollar a day. Each year nearly 8 million children die because of diseases linked to dirty water and air pollution, 50 million children are mentally or physically damaged because of inadequate nutrition, and 130 million children (80 percent of them girls) are denied the chance to go to school.

In spite of improvement in the economy of many regions of the world, food security is a major issue and currently more than 800 million people do not get adequate quantity and quality food because of political, economic, social, ecological and technological problems. These people are mainly in the countries with high levels of poverty and limited social and economic progress. In poor countries poverty has a direct negative implication on their development and widespread poverty in these countries put them at risk of serious social issues. Nearly 40 percent of the people living in developing countries are younger than 15 years, and for countries such as China, India, Indonesia, Nigeria, Pakistan, Bangladesh, Ethiopia, and Egypt, the challenges of population growth will be particularly daunting.

A finally the trend threatening humans are also the physical condition of the earth, which is deteriorating. The earth is getting warmer and because of deforestation the capacity of soils and vegetation to absorb and store water is reduced. Soil erosion by water and wind due to inappropriate agricultural techniques make improvement in the food security a more difficult task.

There is no doubt that the demand for food will increase significantly in the future. Although the Food and Agriculture Organization of the United Nations (FAO) try to distribute enough, safe, and nutritious food to all males and females at any age around the world, experts think that expanding populations need a doubling of food output in the next thirty years. Nevertheless, many experts in the field debate about food deficits at the level of panic. In their view, during the next thirty years productive capacity of the earth suffices to feed everyone. They do not anticipate major climatic changes, at least not for the next thirty to forty years. They think most of the recent problems in the world are human-made famines caused by wars and civil strife. Optimist scientists do not agree with the Malthus theory and think he underestimated the dynamics of technological progress. They also argue that the reforms in agricultural policy in developing countries can at least for the next 30 years produce enough food for their people.

Even if we assume that everything will be favorable for developing countries, soon, many developing countries that were previously agricultural exporters will become importers. Finally, shortage of foreign currency in all these countries, even those which already have resources (most oil—rich countries), will be the major problem of the world and many regions cannot simply buy their food. Overall food is one of the most important needs of any human population and food insecurity is linked to every other facet of the development predicament.

Poverty is the root cause of chronic hunger and struggles between nations. Poverty is not only linked to national economic performance but also to political structure of the countries. The strategy for population control and food security varies from nation to nation, but the leadership of good and constructive governments in a peaceful environment may be able to somehow improve them.

In conclusion, in this chapter we generally discussed population and factors, which influence its size. We have explained that in spite of population control programs in the majority of countries around the world, still the populations of human on earth are rising. Increase in the population directly is associated with demand for more food. We also explained that the food security for a growing world remains an unsolved problem. Even if we were optimistic about our future in the next 30 years, humans will finally face a food shortage. In the following chapters we will see that food by itself is not the only problem, which humans are facing. Energy shortage, environment pollution, moral and political problems, and thousands of other issues should be seriously considered. In this chapter we discussed developed and poor countries. To give an idea about the vast differences between different populations on the earth, in the following table the United States, which is overall ranked number 3 out of 174 countries, will be compared with Bangladesh, which is ranked 146. It should be noted that we only compare a few parameters related to these two populations. Also, it should be noted that several countries such as Afghanistan, which is now in the war with the United States, is not even in the list due to lack of statistics. We will later use these data to predict what will happen to humans in the future if we do not address the world's existing problems soon.

Table 1 (data is not updated).

#	Parameters		The United States	Bangladesh
1	Human Development	Life expectancy 1995 - 2000	76.7 years	58.1 years
		Infant mortality 1998/ 1000	7	79
		Maternal mortality 1990-1998/100,000	8	440
2	Health Profile	Doctors/100,000 (1995)	245	18
		Nursus/100,000 (1995)	878	5
3	Education Profile	Primary (1997)	99.9%	75.1%
		Secondary (1997)	96.3%	21.6%
4	Access to Information	PC/1000 (1998)	451	?
		Internet host/1000 (1998)	113	0
5	Economic US $ (Billion)	Performance (1998)	7,903	44.2
		Average Ann. Inflation	1%	5.3%

6	Macroeconomic Structure US $ Billion GDP	1998	8,230.4	42.7
7	Resource Flows % GDP	Export (1998) Import (1998)	12.1% 13.5%	13.8% 18.9%
8	Resource Use % GDP	Public Expenditure on Education (1997) Public Expenditure on Health (1998) Military Expansion (1998)	5.4 6.5 3.2	2.2 1.6 1.6
9	Aid Flow	Total, million US $, 1998	8,786	0
10	Aid and debt by recipient country	Million, US $, 1998	0	1820.3
11	Demographic Trends	Population, 1998 Population growth, 1998	274 million 1%	124.8 million 2.1%
12	Energy Use	Electricity consumption Total KW, 1997	3,610,149	12,820
13	Environmental Profile	CO2 emission, 1996 Share of the total world Paper consumed 1996 Kg/ capita	22% 145.9	0.1% 1.1

14	Managing the environment	Protected area, 1999 (% national territory)	13.1%	?
		Nuclear waste, 1998 (metric tons heavy metal)	2,700	?
		Hazardous waste generated, 1991-1997 (1000 metric tons	172732	?
		Recycle (% of consumption) 1992-1997		?
				?
		Paper	41%	?
		Glass	26%	
15	Food Security and Nutrition	Supply of calories 1997	3,699	2,085
		Supply of proteins 1997 (total grams)	112	45
		Food import (1998)	5%	15%
16	Job Security	Unemployment 1998	6,204,000	?
17	Profile of Political life	Voters turnout at latest election	36%	?
18	Crime	Total/100,000 in 1994	5,367	?

19	Personal Distress	Road accidents per 100,000 in 1997	1,266	?	
		Suicide male 1993-1998 per 100,000	19	?	
			5	?	?
		Suicide female 93-98 per 100,000	49%	?	
			11,539	186,935	
		Divorces 1996 (% of marriage)			
		Dead by disaster (total 1980-1999)			
20	Gender Education	Female tertiary students/ 100,000 (1994-1997)	5,847	129	
21	Gender Economic Activity (age> 15 years)	Female as per cent male 1998	79.9%	76.2%	

? = Not known

116

CHAPTER TEN

Humans and Energy

The two concepts most basic to science are matter and energy. Anything which has mass and takes up space is matter. Energy is the capacity to work and it is something, which cannot be seen. As discussed before, one of the most important characteristics of any living organism is exchange of matter and energy. In other words, all living organism need energy to move, to grow, build up the body and reproduce. The energy needed by all organisms for biological activities is in the form of chemical energy. The main source of chemical energy consumed by living organisms is the sun light. As discussed in chapter three, green plants use this energy in their cells and in the presence of carbon dioxide and water make organic compounds. In other words, the light energy is stored as chemical bonds between carbon atoms as follow.

Energy + 6CO2 + 6 H2O $\longrightarrow$ C6H12O6 (sugar)

Or

Energy + C, C, C, C, C, C, $\longrightarrow$ C-C-C-C-C-C-C

Living organisms use energy stored in the organic compounds by breaking the carbons' bond in a process generally named respiration. In this process carbon and oxygen produce carbon dioxide and energy is released. This means that most carbon atoms used by plants finally get back to the atmosphere for recycle and energy is finally released as heat into the environment. The reaction is as follow.

$$C\text{-}C\text{-}C\text{-}C\text{-}C\text{-}C \longrightarrow C, C, C, C, C, C + Energy$$

In our bodies reaction takes place in the mitochondria, which is an organelle in the cytoplasm of our cells. All organisms, while still alive, need this type of energy to be alive. We receive chemical energy through foods.

In addition to chemical energy humans need other types of energy for maintaining the environment temperature, lightening, transportation, and machinery in agriculture. At present, this type of energy, which is essential for existence of humans on earth, is so important that we consider it as a major part of our lives. In other words, without this second form of energy more than 90 per cent of human activities will be absolutely stopped. The second type of energy is produced by various methods generally categorized as, nuclear energy, geothermal energy, hydroelectric energy, solar energy, fossil energy, and energy produced by the wind. Energy produced by anyone of the above methods is finally converted to electrical energy, which is used, by more than 95% of humans. In this book the details and methods used for production of energy will not be discussed; however, in only one sentence it can be mentioned that none of the above types are energy are as efficient as fossil energy i. e., coal, natural gas and oil. Energy is the basis of industrial civilization and without it continuation of modern life is impossible. Oil, a form of fossil is the cheapest and the easiest form of energy source and is now the most favored type of energy. Fossil fuels (coal, oil, and natural gas) are the primary source of energy in western countries. In the United States about 85 percent of current US fuel comes from fossil fuels.

Early humans mainly used wood as the major source of energy because it was readily available in the forests around the world and the total need for heating and cooking was relatively very low. In the past, in certain parts of the world other types of material such as coal were also used as energy sources. During the Middle Ages humans learned how to make charcoal from wood. They also learned methods to use the heat produced by charcoal to break up chemical compounds and produce certain metals. Gradually, in the 18th century and during the Industrial Revolution, charcoal was replaced by coke (produced from coal). In addition to home use, coal was also used to drive steam engines in the 18th century and gradually became the dominant energy source. Although for many years crude oil (petroleum) had been used in small quantities, the actual petroleum use began when an oil well was used in the production of oil in Pennsylvania in 1859. After this event, the oil production in the United States expanded rapidly and oil companies soon began exporting oil to all areas of the world. During the 19th century with the development of the internal-combustion engine and the automobile a new product named gasoline was produced from crude oil and gradually oil replaced coal. Intensive need for oil forced other countries such as Britain, the Netherlands, and France to search for oil in many parts of the world, especially the Middle East. The British started to produce oil in Iran just before World War I (1914-1918) but the United States was still the main country in the business of the oil production. At the end of the World War I, the United States was the main oil importer in the world for a few years. Gradually, the oil companies were formed in the United States, Britain and France and the oil business expanded for several years. The companies started to provide increasing quantities of cheap oil for only a dollar per barrel (42 gallons). Of course, the United States remained a self-sufficient country for oil and its need was secured up to 1960. In 1960 big western oil companies cut oil prices, therefore, the governments of the major oil-exporting countries formed an organization named OPEC (Organization of Petroleum Exporting Countries) to confront the low oil price. The main members of OPEC at its onset were countries in the Persian Gulf area. However, the OPEC was successfully formed but could not increase the oil price significantly. In the meantime, the oil consumption drastically increased all over the world especially in Europe and Japan. High demand for oil caused the energy crisis in 1973. In this year as a result of the Arab-Israeli War, the Arab oil-producing countries stopped production of oil shipments to the United States and the Netherlands and their action created oil panic in the world. Gradually, new countries joined OPEC and raised the price of crude oil to eight times high and most OPEC governments took over the ownership of their oil fields. The second oil crisis was in 1978 when the revolution the in Iran drove the Shah of Iran from his throne. Experts believe that the main reason for revolution in Iran, which resulted in the second oil crisis, was the first oil crisis and an increase in the oil price lead by Shah of Iran. Since that time Iran was the major exporter of oil the revolution in Iran for a period of time forced up oil prices. The war between Iran and Iraq in 1980 affected the oil production and prices even more and at the end of 1980 the price of the crude oil was 19 times more than ten years earlier. The high oil prices caused a worldwide recession but gradual increases in the oil production by non-OPEC countries brought the oil prices lower. The third crisis of oil was in 1990 after Iraq's invasion of Kuwait.

Crude oil and natural gas are found in large quantities in more than 50 countries in all parts of the world. The Middle East countries have more than half of the known oil reserves and one-third of the known natural-gas reserves. The United States contains only about 2 percent of the known oil reserves and 3 percent of the known natural-gas reserves. At present, the world's technically recoverable reserves of the crude oil are about 1,000 billion barrels, of which some 73 billion barrels are in North America. By 1999, the United States was using 7 billion barrels of petroleum per year, and worldwide consumption of petroleum was 27.4 billion barrels per year. This means that the United States alone uses about 26 percent of the oil in the whole world. Now we can predict the problem in the world. Since nearly 2/3 of the world's oil reserves are in the Persian Gulf and Caspian Sea (South and north of Iran) this part of the Middle East is the most sensitive part of the world and is the major concern for the western countries, especially the United States, which depends on this oil. The western countries are really concerned about the possible fourth oil crisis, which can be devastating and even worse than the previous ones. This is why experts are uncertain about future oil production and its price. Meanwhile the demand for oil is increasing. Scientists believe that the world oil supply will be around 80 million barrels per day in 2010 to 2020. The world oil consumption was about 70 million barrels per day in 1998.

Despite high reserve of natural gas in the Middle East and Russia, western countries are not very interested in the Natural gas due to the fact that its transport to the west is not as easy as oil. Later we will discuss the issue of oil in the world and will see that one of the major causes for problems in the Middle East and the relation of countries in this region with the United States is oil.

Oil is used for production of gasoline, kerosene, diesel oil, jet fuel, home heating oil, heavy fuel oil, lubricants, and starting material for petrochemicals. In other words, it is used for maintaining temperatures in homes, offices, factories, and industrial facilities. Its derivatives are also used for transportation, in industry and agriculture. This means that shortage of oil in the world even for a short time could put all western countries especially the United States into real kais.

It should be noted that despite its high price, the price of crude oil is still too low. For example, the price of one-gallon of crude oil is ½ of what one gallon of bottled drinking water costs in California. Nevertheless, scientists are searching for a cheaper source of fuel, which does not occur in nature. These days' synthetic fuels are made from cheap natural materials. At present, it is possible to manufacture alcohol fuels but the cost and benefit is still under question. Therefore, synthetic fuels are unlikely to make an important contribution to the world's energy problem soon. Even compared to oil, a relatively cheap source of energy on the earth is coal. Coal is a term used for solid materials that are high in carbon contents. Electric utility companies to produce steam for generators use most coals. Due to certain environmental problem, which will be discussed in chapter 11, the use of coal is limited despite its vast reserves (five times more than crude oil) in the world. The amount of coal (as measured by energy content) that is technically and economically recoverable under present conditions is five times as large as the reserves of crude oil. One -fourth of the world's recoverable coal reserves are in the United States. Overall, the industrialized countries are built on the oil energy and these countries, which use most of the oil in the world, are highly dependent on cheap oil. The United States needs for crude oil is dependent on foreign sources of oil and this country does whatever is needed to protect it. The war between Iraq and Kuwait in 1990 is a good example. In this war, US troops were sent to the Persian Gulf in part to guard against a possible cutoff of oil supply. Although this war is over now, the United States still spend billions of dollars for protecting oil supplies in this part of the world. At present the reliance of the United States on the Middle East oil is about one-third of its total use. It is predicted that if everything stay as it is, by 2030, the United States may be relying on the Middle East oil for two-thirds of its supply. In a sentence, in business usually producers are after customers but this general role is not applied to oil. In the oil business, customers are after producers and do whatever is needed to protect their interests.

What is oil? Crude oil (petroleum) is a bituminous liquid composed of various organic chemicals. It is found below the surface of the earth. Although the derivatives of crude oil are used in the production of certain alcohols, detergents, synthetic rubber, glycerin, fertilizers, sulfur, solvents, and the feed stocks for the manufacture of drugs, nylon, plastics, paints, polyesters, food additives and supplements, explosives, dyes, and insulating materials, humans use the refined oil and its derivatives primarily for transportation, petrochemical industry, generating electricity, and agriculture. In the recent years the worldwide availability of petroleum has steadily declined and its relative cost has increased. The main chemical composition of crude oil is hydrocarbons. Hydrocarbons are organic compounds mainly consisting of carbon and hydrogen. The carbon atoms are in the form of chain (-C-C-C-). In the presence of oxygen, the carbons' bonds break and energy is released. Crude oil also contains gaseous elements. When larger quantities of gaseous compounds are present, the petroleum deposit is associated with a deposit of natural gas. Crude oil was formed under the earth's surface millions of years ago by the decomposition of tiny marine organisms. The deposits of these organisms, which were rich in organic materials, become the source of crude oil and natural gas. In order to find crude oil, geologists must search for a sedimentary rock where organic material has been buried into porous traps under the ground. To find crude oil and then drill the potential areas, geologists and geophysicists need many different tools. Once the crude oil has been produced in the oil fields, it is treated with certain chemicals and then is stored in tanks. Later it is transported to a refinery. Large oil fields all have direct outlets to major common-carrier pipelines. It should be noted that in spite of high reserves of oil in the Middle East, countries in these regions are either completely or partially dependent on developed countries mainly in the west to find, drill, transport and refine the crude oil for them. In other words, the knowledge and tools needed for nearly all stages of oil production is in the hand of developed countries.

As noted above, the world's oil reserves are limited. It is likely that some additional discoveries maybe made in the coming years but the final scenario is the fact that oil will be finished soon. We know that at present more than 90 percent of total income of many oil producing countries is related to selling oil to industrial countries. Unfortunately, most of these countries do not have any plan for their future and one can guess what will happen to them when their oil reserves run out. Considering the reserves available, it is apparent that humans should search for an alternative energy source to sustain the civilized societies of the world in the future. Although alternative energy sources, such as geothermal energy, solar energy, wind energy, and nuclear energy (fission) hold promise, but none of them are an economically viable replacement for the oil products.

Perhaps energy obtained from fusion of hydrogen atoms in coming years will solve the energy issues in the world.

Finally, increasing international demand for the oil proves that oil is a valuable commodity. For rich OPEC countries, their oil imports bring them tremendous annual wealth. In fact the political capacity and stability of these nations depend only on oil.

In summary, in this chapter we learned that humans need for energy is as important as food and without a cheap source of energy, the existence of humans is in jeopardy. At present energy obtained by burning oil derivatives are the cheapest and the easiest form of energy. Over fifty percent of total known oil reserves of the world are in the Middle East regions and western countries especially the United States depend on the oil from this part of the world. No matter what humans do in the future the oil reserves in the world will run out of oil. Humans should either soon find an alternative source of energy or be ready for real disaster in the coming years.

CHAPTER ELEVEN

Human and Environment

As discussed before the beginning of life and its existence on the earth depend on several physical and chemicals factors such as, the presence of water, atmosphere (oxygen, nitrogen, and carbon dioxide), soil, and desired temperature. It is obvious that changes in these physical and chemical factors directly affect the living organisms on earth including humans. Where all organisms live is called environment. In other words, all external factors affecting an organism are the environment for that organism. These external factors can be other organisms or factors such as water, soil, climate, light, carbon dioxide, and oxygen. In a given region, all interacting factors are named an ecosystem. In an ecosystem, organisms are always interacting with their environment and it is in fact the environment, which limits the size of population. Humans can adapt themselves to different environments and therefore they are practically all over the world. They are also the only species on earth, which have the most effect on the environment and the earth. Scientists try to understand the long-term effect of humans on the environment and find methods to control the impact of human activities on the natural world. Ecologists study the relation between organisms and their environments and try to explain why an organism lives in a certain place. The population of different organisms cannot grow forever. In other words, the environmental factors eventually limit population growth in all living organisms. In an ecosystem, all species directly or indirectly interact with each other and extinction or abnormal growth of a species in an ecosystem may affect other organisms in the same region. In other words, species, which live in an ecosystem, establish a balance between themselves.

Humans were always aware about their close interactions with the environment. They also knew that their activities have a direct effect on the environment. Perhaps we should quote Henry David Thoreau (1817-1862), the American naturalist who said,"Thank *God, men cannot yet fly and lay wasteto the sky as well as the earth.*" In 1864, George Perkins Marsh, in his book, *"Man and Nature"*, demonstrated that humans' activities could cause dramatic and irreversible damage to the earth. Marsh explained the effect of agricultural on deforestation, loss of wetlands, desertification, species extinction, and weather changes.

Increase in knowledge about the environment and needs for environment protection gradually resulted in the creation of law for conservation of natural resources in the developed countries. During his presidency (1901 to 1909), Theodore Roosevelt expanded the limit of national forest and national park systems in the United States and created a system of national wildlife refuges. During this time, it was believed that the resources in the United States should be used for the betterment of the American people. Roosevelt thought that one of the most valuable assets in any country is the people themselves and therefore they should be protected. Rachel

Carson perhaps presented the real warning about the effect of humans on the environment in 1962. In a book named, *Silent Spring*, she discussed the worldwide dangers posed by using DDT (dichlorodiphenyltrichloroethane) and other pesticides. Carson argued that humans and wildlife were at risk because of too much DDT present in the environment. Gradually activists in the field brought up the subject of environmental protection and their efforts caused establishment of Earth Day in 1970. Later, other organizations such as the Environmental Defense Fund (1967), Friends of the Earth (1968), Greenpeace (1970), the Natural Resources Defense Council (1970), and the Sierra Club Legal Defense Fund (1971) were gradually established to deal with environment protection. Attention was especially given to air pollution control in 1970 by establishing the national environmental quality standards. This was followed by passing Clean Water Act in 1972. The Resource Conservation and Recovery Act (RCRA), adopted in 1976 aimed protection of human health and conserving valuable natural resources. A part of this act is related to controlling hazardous waste and a recycling program. The issue of environmental protection in the United States gradually caused interest in this subject internationally and monitoring global pollution was developed worldwide. One of the most important achievements of humans regarding the environment is possibly creation of the United Nations Environmental Program (UNEP). One of the main policies of the UNEP is improving standards of living for humans without damaging the environment in developing countries.

In 1992, the UN Conference on Environment and Development discussed two major environmental issues i.e., reduction of emission of gases which cause global warming, and protection of endangered species and habitats. Although the results of this conference was not equally accepted by all countries around the world, today we know that saving the environment is a very important issue on earth. We also know that pollution; destruction of the world's rain forests, global warming, uncontrolled population growth and the depletion of the ozone layer will be the major problems for earth in the coming years. Uncontrolled population growth is possibly the most important environmental problem. Increase in the number of people in the world means more pollution, more destruction, and a decrease in the natural resources. As discussed before, the human population will reach to about 10 billion in 2025. Now, one can assume what will happen to the earth in the coming years. Studies showed that the main factors, which may be able to some degree, adjust the population growth, are democracy and social justice in the communities. Studies also showed that increase in literacy rates caused more productive birth control and family planning.

The major factors affecting the environment are global warming, energy production, Ozone Layer depletion, air pollution, water pollution, chemicals, habitat destruction and species extinction, living zone and wastes. Here each one of these subjects will be briefly discussed.

1. Global warming

Certain gases such as carbon dioxide, methane, and nitrous oxide increase the heat on the surface of the earth by preventing escape of the sun's radiation from the earth, something that is referred to as the greenhouse effect. These gases keep the favorable temperature on the earth and prevent freezing by warming the earth. This means that increase in the concentration of these gases in the atmosphere causes increase in the temperature, which is referred to as global warming. During the last century, the amount of carbon dioxide in the earth's atmosphere has increased mainly due to burning fossil fuels. Increase in the atmosphere temperature causes rise in the sea levels (due to ice melting), which consequently destroy many coastal cities around the world. In the future, it will also cause destruction of agriculture and increase in the frequency of hurricanes and droughts.

2. Energy production

As discussed before, humans are highly dependent on the energy obtained from burning fossil fuels, especially oil. Also, in chapter 10 it was mentioned that the global reserves for fossil fuels are limited, when used, the fossil fuels produce several gases including carbon dioxide and increase the amount of carbon dioxide in the atmosphere causing global warming, air pollution, and acid rain. It seems the easiest way to stop this environmental issue is using nuclear energy. The energy obtained by fission is useful for production of electricity; however, it has its own problems. The use of uranium in nuclear reactors produces radioactive waste, which by itself is highly dangerous. Radiations emitted by radioactive materials are carcinogenic. Using other sources of energy such as solar energy and wind energy may be the second choice but they are not as efficient as oil energy. It seems the best and the most efficient type of energy production on earth in the coming years will be fusion (what happens on the sun). Unfortunately, humans could not control this reaction (fusion) up to now. Perhaps new scientific findings in the future will solve this issue.

3. Ozone Layer depletion

A region of the atmosphere about 35 kilometers above the earth's surface is called the Ozone layer. In this layer three oxygen atoms form molecules and serve as a shield holding ultraviolet (UV) rays, which reach earth from the sun. As discussed before, UV radiation can produce ions and overall is carcinogenic. In the 1970s, scientists discovered that this layer could be destroyed by chlorofluorocarbons (CFCs), a gas which is mainly used in refrigeration and aerosol sprays. The rate of ozone depletion at the present time is out of limit and the consequences of depletion of Ozone layer will finally lead to many serious problems on the living organisms on earth.

4. Air Pollution

A present nearly all industries and transportations in the world depend on the burning of fossil fuels. Burning fossil fuels produces small molecules containing carbon, sulfur, and nitrogen and these molecules contribute to air pollution. In the presence of UV radiations, many dangerous molecules are formed in the atmosphere which overall are referred to as smog. The sulfur dioxide and nitrous oxide produced in the atmosphere finally transfer into sulfuric and nitric acids, which come back to earth in the form of acid rain. Acid rain causes acidic condition in the lakes and destroys the forest ecosystems worldwide.

5. Water pollution

Water is one of the main components for the existence of life on earth. In the world, there are about 1.5 billion people who do not have access to   safe drinking water and at least 5 million deaths per year are related to waterborne diseases. Water pollution is the result of contact between factories wastes, pesticides, fertilizers and untreated sewage with water. Water pollution contributes serious damage to marine wildlife and human health.

6. Chemicals

Each day humans release many kinds of chemicals into the environment. Of these chemicals, especially pesticides and mercury are very important and cause serious damage. A trace amount of a number of these chemicals causes cancer, birth defects, and mutations. Studies show that the number and the amounts of these chemicals are significantly high now and are increasing every year.

7. Habitat Destruction and Species Extinction

It is obvious that air pollution, water pollution, and chemicals in the environment will negatively affect all organisms on earth. Many organisms of different species die each year due to drastic changes in the environment, which are mostly caused by human activities. The main reason for extinction of species is habitat destruction.

8. Living zone

People around the world are not equally exposed to all different changes in the environment. Obviously, people in the poor countries are exposed to toxic materials more than those in the rich countries. Even in a geographic region, not all members of the community are equally affected by air or water pollution. Unequal exposures to the environment changes may in long-term affect the balance between species and individuals in one species. To prevent this type of damage in the communities, authority should consider essential environmental factors before expanding the cities all around the world.

9. Solid Waste

Solid or semisolid materials, resulting from animal and human activities are another potential factor affecting the environment. Unwanted or hazardous wastes classified as: garbage, rubbish, ashes, debris from trees, dead animals, sewage debris, industrial wastes, mining wastes, and agricultural waste. A part of waste materials such as plastics, glass, and paper can be recycled. A number of countries have effective recycling programs but the majority of countries do not have such a program. Since some parts of the waste materials do not degrade, humans release everyday millions of tons of waste to the environment and this will be a problem in the future.

10. Green house

The greenhouse effect is the process by which certain gases in Earth's atmosphere trap heat, keeping the planet warm enough to sustain life.

Here's a deeper look at how it works and why it matters:

How the Greenhouse Effect Works

- Solar radiation reaches Earth as sunlight, mostly in the form of shortwave energy.
- Earth's surface absorbs this energy, warming up, and then emits it back as infrared radiation (longwave energy).
- Greenhouse gases in the atmosphere—like *carbon dioxide* (CO_2), *methane* (CH_4), *water vapor* (H_2O), *nitrous oxide* (N_2O), *and ozone* (O_3)—absorb and re-radiate this infrared energy.

- Some of this re-radiated energy returns to Earth's surface, warming the lower atmosphere and surface more than it would be otherwise.

Why It's Important

- Without the greenhouse effect, Earth's average temperature would be around -18°C (0°F), far too cold for most life forms.
- It's a natural and essential process, but human activities—especially burning fossil fuels and deforestation—have increased greenhouse gas concentrations, intensifying the effect.
- This enhanced greenhouse effect leads to *global warming*, disrupting weather patterns, melting ice caps, and threatening ecosystems.

Key Greenhouse Gases

Gas	Source	Impact on Warming
Carbon Dioxide	Fossil fuels, deforestation	High
Methane	Agriculture, landfills, fossil fuels	Very High
Water Vapor	Natural, amplifies warming	Variable
Nitrous Oxide	Fertilizers, industrial processes	High
Ozone	Chemical reactions in the atmosphere	Moderate

In summary, in this chapter the relation between humans and their environment was discussed. It was clearly shown that many changes in the environment are due to uncontrolled activities of humans. At present, the problems facing the environment are vast and diverse. The effect of environmental change on life on earth is in a critical level now and if we do not control the factors destroying our environment, we will defiantly face serious disaster and permanent damage in the coming years.

CHAPTER TWELVE

Humans and Governments

Discussing the government will be better understood if we evaluate a social system in an animal community as a model. The social behavior of all animal species has evolutionary bases. Nearly all-animal communities have specific rules and taboos and their behaviors to some degrees are associated with their environments. Animals usually form their communities in the areas, which are rich in food with desired physical conditions. They usually assign a border for their communities and somehow mark the limits of their territories. In an animal community usually one and rarely more than one member is superior and this member, who is mostly a strong male, by force govern the community. Obviously, if the members of an animal community face any danger or their territory becomes invaded by another species or even new members of the same species, they get involved in fighting. Human behaviors in their communities are more organized than of other animals because humans are more sophisticated.

During evolutionary process, humans built up structural societies with government, laws and cultural values. Also, during the history, gradually humans added other factors such as religions to their communities to enforce certain behavior. Although a group of scientists believe that social and cultural institutions of humans make them unique and different from other animals but real scientific studies actually prove that humans not only act like animals but in some cases their performance is even worse than animals. Humans usually establish their communities in places, which are rich in food, water, and have desirable environmental conditions. They always have their own territories, which is called states or countries. If another community, especially from its own species, invade their territories and pass their artificial border, they get involve in wars. Usually, one or a group of individuals (mostly males) govern the community. In other words, their governments are super powers and can do whatever they want. Overall, human behaviors do not differ from those of animals. In this chapter the relation between humans and their governments will be discussed. Attempt will be made to show how in certain community's humans do not follow even their own laws and consequently create problems. We will investigate the roots of issues, which humans are facing now.

What is a government? A government is a political system comprising of several individuals, which form institutions in a human population. These institutions are responsible for public policies and conduct affairs of the community. Governments also regulate the relations between different political entities. Sometimes a government has several sub governments but the major decision about the whole community or in other words, the country is made by the main government (in the United States by the federal government). Governments are also responsible for keeping the integrity of the communities and controlling the borders of their communities. Governments are usually classified in many different categories; however, they can generally be classified as dictatorship, monarchy, republic, democratic and fascist. It should be noted that this type of classification is not universal and vary among the nations of the world. Generally, the real functions of the governments are securing territorial, social and economic conditions in the communities. Unfortunately, this is not true in all communities and many of recent problems in the world have roots in corrupted governments.

The history of government goes back to empires of Sumer, Assyria, Persia, Egypt, and Macedonia. In these old civilized communities, cities and states were formed and each state had its own government system which was responsible for imposing the rules of law. Although, the leaders of the governments in these societies were not actually elected by people but officials responsible in different parts of the communities were chosen by citizens of the states. Greeks were possibly the first population who provided the material for the political systems, something that subsequently influenced political thoughts for centuries. Aristotle divided governments into three categories: monarchy, government by a single individual; aristocracy, governed by a select few; and democracy, government by many. Later the governments were classified as: tyranny, rule by an individual who runs the country by his/her own interest; oligarchy, rule by a few people in their own interest; theocracy, rule by religious leaders; and bureaucracy, the excessive domination of government in the administration. The idea of ancient Rome, which finally evolved to governments in the western countries, was a republic form of a government. The Roman concept of the government was alive for a period of time and before influence of the Roman Catholic Church that was followed by monarchy in most parts of the civilized nations of the time.

In 1688 the power of monarchy was restricted in England and parliament was established. Two historic events, American

Revolution (1775) and, French Revolution (1789) had major effects on the rise of modern democratic governments. The history of governments in the 19th and early 20th century is mostly related to reforms in the existing government in the world. Gradually, governments got involved in administering justice, public and social services.

One most outstanding development in the governments in the 20th century was the appearance of proletarian dictatorship in the Union of Soviet Socialist Republics (USSR). However, several eastern European countries formed governments like that of the USSR but, finally this idea became a part of history at the end of the 1980s.

Although in the history of mankind, in many communities past religious leaders acted as governments for a period of time but in recent years the revolution in Iran in 1979 led by Ayatollah Ruhollah Khomeini created a new form of government in the world. The revolution in Iran replaced the monarchy with an Islamic republican system. According to Khomeini's ideas, the government should follow the rules of God and the country (Iran) has to follow Islamic disciplines forced by the supreme spiritual leader. In the following pages we will discuss the outcome of the revolution in Iran and its consequences on the other countries in the Middle East.

The overall structure of the governments in different countries varies but generally governments have three branches named executive, judicial, and legislative. Although in a normal condition these branches are working independently, in a well-organized government they should be able to check one another. As noted above, countries around the world have different systems of government. In countries such as the United States a federal political system controls the national and international political system. Countries like Canada, Australia, Brazil, Germany, India, Malaysia, Mexico, Nigeria, and Switzerland have some sort of federalist governments. In these countries smaller political units run states, provinces, or territories. Not all countries have a system like the United States. Most countries around the world have unitary systems that mean the central government has all authority. For example, countries such as Cameroon, Morocco, South Korea, Sweden, France, Italy, Japan, Kenya, Morocco, South Korea, Sweden, and Uruguay are examples of unitary systems. Likewise, there are countries which have kings or queens as leaders but they are only the symbol for the countries and do not have excess political power. A good example for such a government is the United Kingdom.

There are over 175 countries in the world now and this number is increasing each year. In most countries in the world the governments and political systems are different than what most western countries are familiar with. These countries which are mostly in Asia and Africa have a central government and the same usual branches of a government i.e., executive, judicial, and legislative but, the systems in these countries do not work even by their own standards. There are countries in which the kings have the final power on all branches, no matter what people want. Obviously, in these types of governments usually the son of the king becomes the next king after his father's death. Interestingly, the son of the king is usually trained to become the king without him being checked for any personality or behavioral evaluation of any kind. There are countries, which have one- time, elected presidents but the presidents usually act like the kings and the power is usually transferred to the sons of the presidents. In other words, the presidents are permanent leaders. There are countries in which the spiritual leaders have the final authority. This means that no matter what people want, if the leader finds any law against certain religion beliefs, the people's ideas are not valid at all. There are countries, which have only one party, and obviously the single party runs the country. In these countries there are some sorts of elections, which are only formalities. In these systems nobody competes with the already selected leaders. In many countries around the world the son or close relatives of the leaders have the highest possible key positions in the country and therefore in these states the governments are like family businesses. There are yet countries, which frequently have coup d' etat. In such a country usually an army general becomes the head of the state and after few years change 'his" title to the president and finally is overthrown by another coup d' etat. There are countries in which their political leaders are killed by oppositions before they even talk about reform in the country. Finally, there are countries, which have several leaders. In these countries, the president who is, true or false, "elected" by the people approves a law but the top leader who has the full power refuses to enforce the president's idea.

What were explained above are only examples of different types of governments around the world and I think readers can easily find an example for each one of these systems. What about freedom in these countries? In many countries around the world the word "freedom "does not mean anything. In other words, the leaders of several countries around the world possibly do not know the meaning of this word. In most of these countries the leaders also have full power on the countries' wealth. A significant number of these countries are very poor and rely on the help from other wealthy countries. This means that to receive the financial help, they have to offer some sort of political opportunities. Of course, several countries with unusual leaders have natural resources, for example oil. In these countries things are different. These countries are usually attracted by other rich industrial countries for cheap products such as oil. Obviously, the total income of these nations is under the control of a small number of people who run the countries. Usually, a significant amount of these huge incomes does not even enter the countries and are directly or indirectly transferred to the bank accounts of certain people in the foreign states such as Switzerland. We sometimes hear that a leader of a certain unstable country left the power with billions of dollars and escaped to another country. Some part of the wealth in such countries is spent on preparing food and other essential foreign products to keep their nations quiet. Needless to say that international organizations know that these things happen in some parts of the world but they either do not want to do anything or cannot do anything to resolve the problems.

Now, what is the consequence of having a corrupt government? Let us analyze the condition of the people in countries with corrupt or unpopular governments. Up to 30 years ago, the leaders of the most undeveloped countries could do whatever they wanted and could by force run their states. During the last three decades, with improvement in communication and partial increase in the knowledge of people all around the world people in these nations gradually got some sense about things that were happening around them. Television programs started to broadcast western type of programs all over the world, the term "human rights" was brought up by certain nations, and faxes, radios and recently emails transferred the news around the world in a matter of seconds.

The technology gaps between western countries, especially the United States, and other parts of the world got wider. The consequences of these changes drastically affected on the people in the certain nations. The people in certain nations with rich histories got interested in the future of their nations. To the best of my knowledge, people in these nations became divided in four major groups. (1) The first group who were the top educated individuals in these countries and most of them were educated in the western countries could not resist the unfair situations in their nations and left their homeland as immigrants or refuges searching for the freedom for themselves and their families. (2) The second group who were also educated preferred to stay in their countries and in their own ways tried to be positive in their own nations. Of course, several of them were either executed or are in prisons because of their opposition. (3) The third group consists of those who are interestingly in the minority. This group by force and terror govern these nations and try to destroy their opposition with terror, long-term prison, and even execution. (4) The fourth group of people in these nations, which included most of the population, while under the pressure of their own governments, did not know what to do and quite simply they are confused. A significant number of people in the fourth group are not educated. I personally had the experience of talking to one of them several years ago. In a few hours trip in one of the Middle Eastern countries I was sitting on a seat in a bus close to someone who hated the United States and was using the phrase "death to America" to emphasize his anger. After a few minutes of conversation, I realized that he thought America is a person not a country. He asked me where America lives. Although this is an extreme example and does not mean anything, it shows what sort of people can be categorized in the fourth group. I think these people are the main individuals who are targeted by opportunist leaders for promotional reasons.

Obviously, leaders of most of these countries, especially in the Middle East, are under tremendous pressure from their nations and therefore they try to somehow make their nations busy. In other words, they try to find another person or country to be blamed for the problems. As discussed above, most of these countries do not have real political systems. The people especially in these countries, mostly young generations, usually get information through television and other forms of communication systems. They see, hear or read about the free world and try to join political parties and be useful in their own lands. Since they cannot join a political party because it does not exist, they are mostly absorbed to other societies. What is a political party? A party consists of a group of people with certain policy, which can gather and share their ideas. Since in many countries in which governments have full power, establishment of political parties are not allowed, or if allowed they are only for show business, the ordinary people join religious groups, where they can gather and talk about what they think without any serious opposition. What is the outcome of such a situation in the nations such as those in the Middle East? In chapter thirteen the relation between humans and religions will be discussed in details. Here we only note that religious leaders always love to have more followers. They really like to gain from any opportunities, which are useful for promotion of their ideas. Obviously, leaders who can absorb most of the people take the controls in their hands and the outcome is appearance of religious governments in the 20th century. The youngest major religion in the world is Islam. As we will discuss later, in Islam religious leader may also govern the nation and enforce the rules of God. Of course, each leader has its own interpretation of the rules and therefore we see different outcomes from a single form of religious government. For example, both Iran and Afghanistan have some sort of religious government but they interpret the Islamic laws differently. The government in Iran is more moderate than Afghanistan. Interestingly, they do not even like each other. We all know that running a country in the 21st century is not a matter of "words" and following the rules, which belong to several hundred years ago. So somehow the people should be kept busy before they even think about the advancement in the human lives in recent decades. Obviously, the best solution is finding an excuse. For a religion like Islam in which the subject of women behavior is a big chapter, drinking alcohol is prohibited and generally the western form of life is not acceptable, the best excuse is western countries and in the top of them the United States. The situation in countries with religious leaders is 100 per cent under the control of the top leaders. It is interesting to point out that the leader is not always one person. There maybe 100 leaders who each one has its own idea on a single subject. They try to disconnect the relation between their nations and other parts of the world but at the same time they love to promote their ideas around the world. We know that in Afghanistan something such as having a television was not allowed or in a more advanced Islamic system such as Iran having receivers used for watching international programs on television are not legally allowed. It should be noted that foreign countries are also somehow responsible for appearance and maintenance of these types of systems in the world.

For example, Afghanistan is a very poor country in Asia. The people of this country have been living in that region of the world for thousands of years. It was the invasion of this country by a super power (USRR), which initiated problems there. What we saw in Afghanistan under Taliban was the consequence of the invasion, which took place several years ago. Another example showing the role of a wrong policy of a super power on the third world countries is the role of the United States in the Middle East war between Arabs and Israel. Islamic leaders use this policy as an excuse to keep their people busy with America. Even the moderate Islamic nations gain from what is going on and try to blame the United States for their own internal problems.

Before ending this chapter, several other issues should be discussed. As noted in previous chapter, the people who were living in the areas, which are now Iran, Iraq, Syria, Turkey, Egypt and Israel, were the early civilizations in the world and all of them have very rich histories. The people in this region of the world are intelligent and therefore understand the position of their nations in the world. Most of the population in this area to some degree dislikes their governments. Most oil—rich countries in the world are in the Middle East yet they are still relatively poor both economically and politically. They know they have problems but they do not know the solution. They think they can solve their problems through Islam therefore they follow whoever uses Islam to fight with the western world. Even with their own standards a person like Osama bin Laden or the Taliban group is not following the actual Islamic rules. They are not even at a level to understand Islam but people choose them as their leaders. Although the role of religions in the societies will be discussed later, here we only mention that people like Osama bin Laden are not even at the level to ask for Jihad. By definition, command for Jihad should be given by the highest leader in an Islamic society not by any member of society.

Since the subject of governments are discussed in this chapter, it should also be mentioned that most disasters facing human beings since their appearances are related to the government or leaders who created wars between nations for their own interests. In the history of mankind, we had and still have the leaders who were or are responsible for many unbelievable and inhuman actions. This issue will be discussed in chapter fourteen. Here we only mention two historical facts showing how a leader can kill thousands of innocent people for reasons only acceptable by the leader himself. Everybody knows that in the World War II millions of people were killed by the most shameful methods only because a group of people decided to punish individuals from certain religions. Or in the Middle East wars, we had and still have a leader who killed thousands of people from his neighboring countries for reasons justified by the leader himself. We know that during the Iran/Iraq and Kuwait/ Iraq wars conventional and chemical weapons killed millions of innocent people. In these wars, Iraq used chemical weapons even against the members of its own country. We also remember how hundreds of oil wells were set on fire to show the power of a leader. Experts estimated that such an action had both financial and environmental impacts on the world for several years.

In chapter six, the subject of human behavior was discussed. We now know that people are not born as criminals. It is mostly the environmental and especially childhood and learning ability of individuals, which finally influence and form the personality of people. We also learned that a significant number of individuals who look normal might have some sort of mental or behavioral disorders. Now imagine if one of these abnormal individuals or even a normal person who is misguided by abnormal individuals become responsible for a very sensitive position in a government. The outcome is clear. Thousands of people will be dead by a decision made by such a person.

We can predict mass killing of innocent people, something that we had seen many times in the history of mankind. One interesting issue related to humans is the fact that for a number of sensitive positions, such as being a pilot, or an astronaut the background and psychological evaluations of the applicants are compulsory. Have we ever heard that a person who may be able to destroy a population or use chemical and biological weapons to kill other humans has been evaluated for any behavioral problems? These are examples of facts that human beings are facing now. Is not it logical to find these people and remove them from their position? Is not it essential to enforce an action after it is proved that a leader has behavioral problems? Should not humans through an international agency remove problematic leaders and bring them to justice?

In summary, in this chapter the subject of governments and different forms of government in the world were discussed. We learned that not all governments and leaders in the world are elected by the member of their nations. At present time most people who run major countries are not popular among their own people. The leaders of several states do not even follow the laws of their own lands. Several leaders have fixed minds and should practice only the law of their religious beliefs. Most of the world's population is living in the countries in which the first principle of the life that is freedom is not known. Every day we witness new wars created by people who do not believe in humanity. Human beings are now in a very critical stage and no matter what we do the problems in the world get bigger and worse. We cannot even have our simple lives. We are even afraid to check our own mails. I think humans may be able to control the present situations in the world by careful investigation of the problems and finding international solutions for the existing problems.

CHAPTER THIRTEEN

Humans and Religions

Homo sapiens, from the early stages of appearance on earth have been fascinated by extraordinary events happening in and around its populations. They were seeing and feeling events such as rain, snow, wind, lightening, thunder, stars, moon, sun, comets, meteors, sun and moon eclipses, and similar unusual events. Interestingly, nearly all of these events exist or take place either in the atmosphere or above the atmosphere. This means that early humans were always searching for some sort of super power in the sky, which according to their knowledge at the time had been responsible for these events. Gradually, different types of super powers were created by them to justify these events. These unknown super powers were later named Gods. These super powers gradually became the center for worship and since most unusual events, for example sun eclipse, were frightening, the early humans started to be afraid of their God's decisions. Later when religions were formed, God became the center of prayer for these events. For example, humans were praying to God for rain to have better and more productive agriculture. Since a number of these events were extremely powerful, humans gradually accepted that God even created them too. Later, God was considered the source of everything including eternity, goodness, knowledge, and power. This type of thinking gradually caused the idea that God is a mystery beyond the understanding of humans and he is responsible for every move of humans. Although during the history of mankind the majority of people believed in the absolute power of God but there were also philosophers and theologians who believed in a limited knowledge for God. Nearly in all religions (see below) God is considered as an independent power over the world including the existence of humans. In certain religions it is believed that God is present within all processes. Also, in certain religions God is the only one individual with a specific personality. On the other hand, some people believe that there are several Gods. In three major religions in the world (Judaism, Christianity, and Islam), which are related to each other the unity for God is conceived. In Judaism, which is older than the other two religions, Jews believe that God is present as a creator and Lord of all the earth. Jewish people believe that God does not have a material image. They think God can be angry; but his primary attributes are justice, mercy, truth, and faithfulness. In Christianity, which began as a Jewish sect, Jesus Christ was probably understood as a prophet of God; however, gradually Christians viewed him as a divine being and a title such as father or lord was used for him to stress his love and care rather than his power. Islam arose as a reaction against the ancient pagan cults of Arabs. Muslims also believe that God is personal, transcendent, unique, and nobody created him. They believe that God has life, knowledge, power, will, hearing, seeing, and speech and everything that happens depends on him.

Despite the differences, the conception of God in Judaism, Christianity, and Islam is more or less the same. The religions in a number of Asian countries have different view of God. In

Hinduism God is not unique and can be understood in several ways. In Hinduism, each god has his or her own function. The three principal gods, Brahma, Vishnu, and Shiva—charged respectively with creating, preserving, and destroying. In Buddhism they view that gods are real, but they are not ultimate. To the follower of this religion, the Buddha figures are cosmic beings. In the Mahayana Buddhism the Buddha himself was transformed into a divine being. In Chinese religions, the ultimate Holy Being seems to have an impersonal order, in Daoism it is the rhythm of the universe, and in Confucianism it is the moral law of heaven.

During history, mankind believed in different types of Gods. In Polytheism belief there were many different holy beings and each one cared for some especial aspect of nature or of human affairs. Polytheism was a common form of religion in ancient Egypt, Mesopotamia, Greece, and Rome. Polytheism was developed from another primitive religion called Animism. In Animism belief, the sense of Holy Being is diffused throughout the environment and it is in a multitude of spiritual forces, some friendly and some hostile.

Generally, the concepts of God have been changing during the history but almost all nations throughout history believed in a Holy Being in some sense; however, people who believed in skepticism, materialism, atheism, and other forms of disbelief have always challenged people's beliefs. During the history of mankind, the arguments against belief in God and the existence of God have always been the subject of discussions in different societies. Some people argue that God cannot be another being therefore it does not exist. Some people believe that the God is not something that exists. They think some people believe in God because of their own experiences, for example, mystical experiences, conversion, and a sense of presence, sometimes visions and verbal communications.

There are individuals who have moral experience about God and through him search for truth, the awareness of finite, suffering and death. There are yet individuals who think people believe in some sort of holy being for self-comfort. Many attempts have been made to prove or disprove the reality and existence of God. In many religions it is said that change requires an agent of change therefore existence of the universe and everything in it, which is a major change, need an agent (God) of change. Still, there are people who ask God himself for change then who or what has been the agent of change for him? In other word, if God caused the creation of everything who created God?

I personally experienced that argument about God and its existence is a complicated subject. I think believing in God is something personal and an act of faith. It is related to personal experience in anybody's life. In other words, believing in God is something, which we experience and learn in our life. It is also something, which is transferred to us as a genetic factor without our knowledge. A child born in a Jewish family will believe in a Jewish God and a child born in a Muslim family will believe in a Muslim God. This is why I ask myself, does a baby who lives in this world for only few hours after its birth have the same God as his parents? If humans actually are transferred to another "world" after death, what will be the difference between a baby who has never learned anything about God before his death and a person who spent most of his life worshiping God? I also ask myself if God indeed exists why a tiny planet like earth has so many different types of Gods. I think there should be only one God for all religions. If this is the case, why are there several forms of religions? So, it seems it is meaningless either to affirm or deny the existence of God because simply speaking nobody knows and will never know what God is or is not.

Now the subject of religions can be discussed. Religions are almost always related to God. In other word, the center of any religion is God. So, for those who do not believe in God talking about any religions is meaningless. In other words, there may be individuals who believe only in God without religions but we cannot find anybody who believes in a religion (at least one of the major ones) without believing in God. People who only believe in God argue that religions are man-made on the earth and there is not ever any relation between God and religions. In other words, they think God is such a powerful "something" in the universe that he does not care if someone eats kosher meat or not. He does not care if someone covers her hair or walks naked on a beach. He does not care if a woman drives a car or only man can do it. He does not have time to check if a person goes to church or not. Interestingly, the numbers of individuals who do not believe in the existence of God are higher in modern recent societies compared to previous societies.

Religion is a sacred engagement and belief in a spiritual reality. Religion has been a part of human's culture and it is a complicated tradition in all nations. Although all religions talk about peace and love, nearly all recent major wars in the world have been associated with religions. In other words, early humans were only fighting for food and territory but recent humans not only fight for food and territory but also fighting for ideology is added to other humans' needs. It is interesting to mention that sometimes two nations of a similar religion get involved in fighting for religious reasons.

Although each religion ultimately ends to one set of beliefs but it seems that people traditions and cultural behavior have major influences on practicing religion. For example, in Islam women should cover their hair but this one rule is interpreted differently in different Islamic cultures. In a number of Islamic countries, women are free to either cover or do not cover their hair. In contrast, there are nations in which all women should cover their hair. There are also extreme conditions like what we saw in Afghanistan, where ladies should be absolutely covered in some sort of bag-shape cover.

The intensity of worship and prayer are also directly associated with traditions in different societies. In a given society, there are individuals who almost always read their religious books and do not engage in any other type of activities. In contrast, there are individuals who cannot even read and understand their religious book because it is not even in their own language. Extreme beliefs in a religion may end up in ignorance, fanaticism, or wishful thinking. Likewise, experience of religions may be expressed by different methods such as visual symbols, dancing, performing, philosophical systems, legendary and imaginative stories, ceremonies, meditations, or other rules. In several nations in the world, a religion may be like an organized institution, which is not a part of its culture, and therefore they do not follow the law and order governed by the society. Sometimes such as scriptures, sacraments, martyr, or cult, which is considered the holiest in a community, may not be important or sacred for another group even in the same religion. Nearly in all religions several principles, such as individual rights, freedom, justice, or equality are claimed. Religious systems are sometimes organized around specific past events occasions or memories. In these cases, the followers try to remember these events by continual renewal of the events. The renewal may take place annually, monthly, weekly, daily, or even hourly. For example, Muslims pray at five different times every day, or in the holy month of Ramadan observe a fast. For Jews, Yom Kippur is a major time of spiritual renewal and for Christians going to church every Sunday, honoring the day of the resurrection of Jesus Christ. Also, religions may establish special places or locations that are different from other places for specific events. These places or sites may be associated with great religious events in the past—for example, the birthplace of the Hindu god Krishna; or the spot where Muhammad journeyed to the heavens (memorialized by the Dome of the Rock in Jerusalem). These places may also be shrines and temples built for gods, for example, the Parthenon in Greece. Holy places may become objects of pilgrimage, such as the Kaaba in Mecca, Saudi Arabia, which is the holiest shrine of Islam. Nearly in all religions certain events such as birth, weddings and funerals are associated with the religions. Religion may also be used for requesting or offering something from or to the spiritual beings. Sometimes the requests are in times of special need, such as illness, drought, or infertility. Most major religions try to distance the followers from impurity such as sin, immorality, and ignorance and lead them toward purity states of soul, spiritual knowledge, wisdom, or even eternal life. Many religions offer love, self-control, compassion, nonviolence, and wisdom.

During the history of mankind, thousands of religious movements emerged around the world. It is interesting to mention that although humans have been on the surface of the earth for many thousands of years nearly all major religions appeared on the earth only between periods of time starting about 5000 to 1400 years ago. In other words, it seems only during this period of time God(s) became interested in humans out of millions of other species on earth. Of thousands of religions, which emerged on earth, several of them are the main ones and cover most of the population on earth. These religions are: Buddhism, Hinduism, Judaism, Christianity, and Islam. It should be pointed out that each one of these religions has several minor branches. These religions appeared in all Asia and the three major ones (Islam, Judaism and Christianity) in the Middle East. Muslim people consider the Prophet Muhammad as the successor to the Jewish and Christian prophets and interestingly the followers of these three related ones are the creators of most of the wars and problems in the recent years (Chapter fourteen). Although each one of these religions has its own rules and laws but they also have several similarities. For example, they all have big chapter about birth (life), death, soul, after death, heaven, and hell. Before discussing each religion, here briefly these topics will be discussed.

As discussed before, the overall activities and the most valuable thing for any living organism is the life of that organism. Obviously, if for any reason these activities stop, the organism is dead. In humans, life starts when a male sexual cell fuses with a female sexual cell in the uterus of the female. Biologically speaking, the single cell that is formed after this fusion (zygote) has all of the genetic material, which is needed throughout his/her life. In other words, from this point a new life starts. If everything goes in a normal way after about nine months a new organism is born and this is called the birth. Although science has 100 per cent proved this process, still different ideas about how God transfer the soul in the body of the new life in a certain time during pregnancy are the main subjects in different religions. According to certain religions, at a specific time during pregnancy a new life starts under God's control. Therefore, destroying the new life (abortion) is not a right decision because it is against God's will. As discussed above, the life starts immediately after the zygote is formed because this cell can perform all activities that are associated with the life. It is this zygote which, after millions of cell divisions and through the cell differentiation processes produces a baby. Despite advanced progress in the biological sciences, such as cloning, stem cell research, and test tube babies, still a number of religions believe that humans should not interfere with God's decision about life. In some cases, this subject becomes so important that even using any type of birth control is not allowed in certain cultures. There are even worse conditions. For example, several religious people in certain religion believe that if the parents of a child are not officially married by a religious leader, this child is not a normal child and may for example become a criminal later in his/her life. After birth, in normal conditions, any human grows, learns from their environment, gets old, and finally dies. Death is an irreversible cessation of life. Death is the final stage of life loss and is one of the essential characteristics of living. Death may occur due to many different reasons but its start is associated with the cessation of heartbeat, respiration, movement, reflexes, and brain activity. It should be mentioned that after this stage for a certain period, depending on the different organs, the cells in the body may be alive but the overall function is dead. The symptoms of death are similar to the state of coma and fainting. The death occurs when the vital functions of the body such as breathing and circulation stop. This is followed by brain death, which is the final sign of death. Recent advancement in the science showed that before final stages of the death it is possible to somehow preserve something from the dead body. In the future, humans may reach to a level that makes them able to preserve the whole body and bring it to the life several years later. This may be useful for the possible journey to other planets in the coming years (chapter 16). After death, several changes such as body cooling, the stiffening of the muscles, and discoloration of the body to reddish-blue occurs. Clotting of the blood in the cardiovascular system begins immediately after death and body cells start to autolysis. The putrefaction and decomposition of body is followed by the actions of microorganisms, especially bacteria, which live in our own body (especially in the digestive system). Not all organs die at the same time. This is why certain organs can be removed from a dead body soon after death and transplanted into other living individuals. Something which is certain is the fact that after a period gradually all components of the body break down by the action of bacteria and fungi that are in or around the body and finally big molecules break down to smaller molecules and even certain atoms which are then available for use in another form of life. Another form of life can be another human several years later. It is possible to preserve the body of a dead person by using certain anti-bacterial and anti-fungal substances (like Egyptian mummies), but this action does not mean that the preserved body gain life later. Such a preserved body may finally ends up being in a museum. This means that "physical" form of any human finally disappears forever. Scientists who studied near death experience in those who died and came back to life concluded that immediately after death several things including denial and isolation, anger, rage, envy, resentment, bargaining, depression, and acceptance occur.

The ideas about death vary in different religions. Some people believe that death starts with departure of the soul from the body. In different societies there are many issues related to death. For example, many people ask: who shall decide somebody's death? Do people have the right to demand their own death? Can a legal guardian permit someone's death? Is it morally right to use human's tissues for transplantation? Is it right to kill terminally ill patients? The discussions related to these questions are out of the subject of this book.

Dealing with the subject of death in different nations is very complicated and cannot be discussed here. In several religions, the body of a dead person should be burned. Some people try to preserve the body but most nations bury dead bodies. Something which is shared by nearly all religions is the belief of the transfer of life to another form of "life" after death. In many religions, it is believed that each human consists of mainly physical parts and a soul. What is soul? The immaterial element that with the material body constitutes the human individual is soul. Generally, soul is considered as something vital, mental, and spiritual. Most cultures believe in the existence of soul apart of the body. Some people even believe that there are several types of souls. In Hinduism the soul is considered as the principle of the controls of all activities. Followers of Buddhism believe that the individual soul is an illusion produced by various psychological and physiological influences. Early Judaism believed in human personality with distinction between body and soul. Jewish people believe that the soul is the principle of life and is able to survive. Most Christians believe that each individual has an immortal soul and each human is composed of soul and resurrected body. The idea of Muslim people about soul is like those of Jewish and Christian. Muslims believe that God breathed the soul into the first human being, and at death the souls of the faithful Muslims go back to God. Overall, in all religions the moral and spiritual experiences of life and soul are associated to the life after death. Do we really come back or go somewhere after death? Those who really understand the life as a whole do not believe in the soul or any return of any sort. To them, soul is billions of organized chemical reactions which take place in our bodies when we are alive. After death, a significant number of these reactions may continue for a certain time in an unorganized form but the outcome is the absolute stopping of all organized reactions in a biological unit. Although it is unlikely for any dead person to return to any form of life after death, it is hard to change the ideas of those who believe in life after death. Now another aspect of life after death will be reviewed. Nearly all major religions believe that there is some sort of judgment (punishment or reward) after death. Of the different beliefs about judgment after death, those that are related to humans transferring to heaven or hell are the most interesting ones.

What is heaven? Generally, in religions, heaven is a place or condition which has all perfect supernatural good things and God, Gods or other spiritual beings that dwell are in there. Those who believe in the existence of such a place think that if our earthy life is absolutely pure, its continuation will be transfer to heaven as a reward. Jewish mystics, based on Persian doctrine, regarded the heavens as seven spheres of the firmament where the new life starts. Some people believe that heaven is a place where mortals might continue the pleasures of earthly life. Christians believe that the souls of those who are free from sin are admitted immediately after death into heaven, where their chief joy consists in an unclouded vision of God. A group of Christians believe that the soul first passes through a stage of purification before entering heaven. Muslims consider the heaven as a happy place with unrestricted and inexhaustible partaking of the joys of physical sense. To some Muslim people, heaven is like a huge beautiful and unbelievable garden with rivers and full of different forms of fruits with many nymphs (*houris of paradise*). Many writers consider this type of heaven allegorical. Overall, heaven is a very relaxing and fantastic place according to certain people beliefs. Does such a place really exist? If we consider heaven as a "physical" place (such as a garden) only physical body can enjoy it.

We already know that our physical bodies convert to soil and the materials used for building our bodies are used first by bacteria and fungi and later through re-cycle events by other form of life. Now imagine two individuals who during their earthly lives used certain atoms both go to heaven, which one of these two individuals will carry those atoms? This means that physical body and physical heaven do not match. If we consider transfer of the soul to a physical heaven, we face an even more complicated problem. What can the soul which is some sort of "energy" do in a place made of materials?

These questions led to another idea which says the soul moves to another place which is not made of materials. We know that there are lots of mysteries in the universe. There may be such a place in the universe but its doubtful existence is not known to humans for sure. Several people who do not believe in the existence of heaven ask: what sort of enjoyments will be offered to a baby who dies one hour after its birth? Such a baby will go to heaven because of its absolute purity. They also ask: what happens to other forms of life on earth? Do they have a chance to go to heaven too? If yes, based on what sort of evaluation and judgments?

What is hell? It is opposite to heaven. Hell is a place or state of punishment for certain human souls after death. In other words, hell is the place or state of eternal punishment of the damned humans. In many religions, existence of hell is something which complete heaven and confirm justice after death. In other words, if someone is not going to go to heaven, he/she should go to somewhere which is 100 per cent opposite to heaven. They think some people do not get a chance to be adequately punished during their earthy life therefore they should be punished in hell. Some people believe that hell is a very hot place with millions of dangerous animals. They think bad people will be constantly punished in hell. A few people believe that continuous physical punishment after death is not something acceptable. The nature of the punishment in hell is not clear for anybody yet. Some people think the punishment in hell is a constant pain. Obviously, those who do not believe in the existence of hell argue and ask: who will be punished? When we talk about pain we think of the physical body. If hell is made of fire, once and for all a physical body will burn out and if only a soul can exist in hell, the type of pain effective on the soul is not clear. Frankly speaking, it seems hell is somewhere like the sun in our solar system.

We have some sense about the major religions; therefore, here the basic principles of each religion will be briefly discussed.

Hinduism: This religion originated in India and many Indians are its followers around the world. Hinduism is one of the major religions in the world with over 700 million followers. This religion had profound influence on the other religions during its long history dated about 1500 BC. Hinduism is some sort of social and doctrinal system that extends to every aspect of human life. It is especially defined by what people do but not what they think. Most Hindus worship Shiva, Vishnu, or the Goddess (Devi), but they also worship additional minor deities. Hindus believe that the universe is a huge sphere, containing heavens, hells, oceans, and continents. They believe that India is at the center of this universe. They think after death, the soul leaves the body and is reborn in the body of another person, animal, vegetable, or mineral. One of the most interesting beliefs of Hindus is their opposition to injury, which justify their vegetarianism. Hindus believe in several Gods; however, most worshipers are devoted to a single God.

Buddhism: this religion was founded in northeastern India by Siddhartha Gautama, who is also known as Buddha. The Buddha rejected significant aspects of Hinduism and opened his philosophy to members of all castes. Buddhism today is divided into two major branches. Buddhism has been significant not only in India but also in Sri Lanka, Thailand, Cambodia, Myanmar and Laos China, Japan, Taiwan, Tibet, Nepal, Mongolia, Korea, and Vietnam. The followers of Buddhism worldwide are estimated at between 150 and 300 million.

Judaism: Judaism is one of the oldest religions which is followed by Jews or people of Israel. According to this religion, God instructed the people of Israel and the worldview and the way of life which are Jewish laws, customs, and practice. Judaism is a system of sanctification in which all God's rules should be followed. Christianity is originated from Jewish ideology and Islam has strong roots in Judaism. Since the 7th century, Jews lived within Christians and Islamic cultures and these two religions had impacts on the history of Judaism. Judaism originated in the present Israel; however, its followers migrated to different parts of the world. At present, the population of Jews is about 13 million and most of them live in the United States (more than Israel), Israel, Russia, France, and Great Britain. This religion is possibly the second (after Islam) most complex religious tradition in the world. They believe in a single God who created the universe and governs it. They also believe that God revealed himself through Moses (Jews' prophet) to the Israelites at Mount Sinai by sending commandments which are in the Torah. The founder of Israel and the prophet of Jewish people (Hebrews) is Moses.

According to Jews, Moses was born in Goshen, a part of ancient Egypt, while Hebrew people lived in Egypt and Pharaoh was the Egyptian ruler. Before the birth of Moses, Pharaoh ordered the death of all Hebrew male infants. Moses was saved by the action of his mother who placed him in a basket and left the basket on the Nile River. Moses was later rescued by the daughter of Pharaoh who adopted Moses as her own child. During his adulthood, Moses killed an Egyptian who had murdered a Hebrew and left Egypt and became a shepherd until he was 80 years old. According to history, Moses went back to Egypt and with Hebrew people left Egypt for the land of Canaan (Palestine) and settled there.

Moses later received the Ten Commandments from Yahweh and thereafter the fundamental laws of the Hebrews and Judaism started. The covenant between God and the Jewish people is a major concept in the Judaism. According to the traditions, God has a special relationship with Jewish people; therefore, Jews acknowledge God as their sole ultimate to obey and God consider them as his particular people. Jewish people believe that the earth belongs to God and Jews must acknowledge God by praying three times a day. They think certain animals such as pigs and fish without fins or scales are not clean and should not be eaten. They also believe that the animals which can be used should be slaughtered and the blood fully drained before the meat (Kosher) can be eaten.

Muslim people have exactly the same ideas. Interestingly, these two religions which have the closest bonds are at present the main center of the wars in the world, something which will be discussed in detail later. Jews also think that meat and milk products should not to be eaten together. According to the Jewish laws at the age of eight days, a male child should be circumcised, another similarity between Jews and Muslims.

In the history of Jews, the exile of the Judeans to Babylonia in 586 BC is a major turning point in Israelite religion. In their history Jewish people consider Cyrus the Great (a Persian king) as a great man because, after conquering Babylon in 539 BC, he permitted the restoration of the local Jewish temple in which a high Jewish priest was its chief administrator. Another interesting issue, at present the government of Israel and the government of Iran (Persia) dislike each other.

Obviously, one of the major events in the history of Jews is the anti-Jewish sentiment that took place during World War II in Europe particularly in Germany. The German reform movement abandoned many Jewish laws and customs, which finally led to the most horrible historical events in the history of mankind (chapter fourteen). Another major event in the history of Jews is the establishment of Israel. After destruction of Jews by Nazi and Holocaust, the modern state (country) of Israel was founded, where Jews considered it as their homeland. Israel is now the center of Judaism and in spite of higher population of Jews in the United States, the American Jews are more Israel-oriented.

Christianity: The center of Christianity is Jesus Christ. What we know about Jesus and Christianity is said by his followers who believed him to be a new prophet. Jesus was born in Bethlehem in Judea. Christians refer to Jesus as Son of God because the ultimate mystery of the universe was called "Father" in the sayings of Jesus. Early followers of Jesus regarded him as the redeemer of all humanity. The principal sources of information concerning Jesus are told in the Gospels of the New Testament of the Bible. Jesus has been a historical figure in the history of mankind and his followers believe that Jesus' life including his love and fellowship should be the basis of human relations. One of the most fundamental components of Christianity is the faith in the Christian community —the church. During early Christianity Jerusalem was the center of the Christian movement up to AD 70 but later it was moved to other places in the Palestine and beyond. Christianity, at its onset, manifested relation to the Jewish faith and the Christian Bible (The holy book of Christian) has Jewish roots. Jesus was crucified by the order of the supreme council of Jews which condemned Jesus to death after he was asked to declare whether he was "Christ, the Son of God". This is why early church blamed Jews for Jesus' execution which took place by Roman. Christian believes that after Jesus' death, the resurrection took place and therefore the resurrection became one of the most compelling doctrines of Christianity. Christians think by rising from the dead, Jesus gave humanity hope for life after death. Christians think "God is love" and the creation of the world and humans were expressions of that love. The followers of this religion are distributed all over the world with as many as 1.7 billion followers. Christianity covers the way one live, a system of belief a tradition. Christians believe that Jesus' life should be followed and love and fellowship should be the basis of humans' relations.

Islam: Islam along with Judaism and Christianity are the last three great monotheist religions which started with the Prophet Muhammad in the early 7th century in Mecca, Saudi Arabia. After its appearance, for nearly a century Arab armies expanded Islam to as far as Spain, the Black Sea, and the Indus. In their wars Arabs defeated the Sassanids of Persia and forced the Byzantines out of eastern Anatolia, the Fertile Crescent, Egypt, and North Africa. The center of Islam was then gradually moved out of the Arabian Peninsula to Syria and Baghdad. During Arabs' occupation of Iran (Persia), the local dynasties in Iran kept the Persian traditions, literatures and court ceremonies alive. Gradually, the main branches of Islam, Shiite and Sunni were established in different part of the Middle East. In the 11th century, European Christians went to war with Muslims in the Mediterranean areas, which finally ended the promotion of trades between Europe and the Middle East.

Muslim people believe in both Christianity and Judaism and worship the God of Jews and Christians. They believe that Muhammad is the last Prophet and he was sent by God to complete all religions. Islam is possibly the most complex religions with many rules and laws. Several Islamic rules are like those of Jewish. They believe that there is only one powerful God who created the universe. Islam says all Muslims are equal before God if they are loyal to God. In Islam there is no different between races or nationality and this is in fact one main reason that in recent years the numbers of its followers are increasing. One of the most rewarding practices for each Muslim is converting a none -Muslim person to Islam, something which can be done only by saying few words. In contrast, if a Muslim change his/her religion from Islam to another religion, he/she committed a sin. The followers of Islam are more than 1 billion in all continents, and it is the fastest-growing religion in the world perhaps because of its doctrine of equality.

At the same time, in recent years, Islam is damaged by its followers more than any other religion. The main reason for such damage is the fact that different Islamic leaders interpret Islamic rules by their own understanding. This may have root in the fact that Islam can also govern the nations and an Islamic leader should enforce the rules of God. About 40 countries, mostly Arab origin, are Muslim. In addition, several non-Arab countries such Indonesia, Pakistan, Bangladesh, Iran, India, Nigeria, former USSR, and China also have significant numbers of Muslims.

The founder of Islam is Muhammad. He was born in Mecca in AD 570 and at the age of 40 started the new religion of Islam. Like other prophets, Muhammad was a mortal man, commissioned by God to deliver the message of humanity to people. The laws and rules of Islam are presented in the Qur'an , the holy book of Islam. According to Muslims, the Qur'an is perfect and completes the previous holy books of God. According to Islam, on Judgment Day people will be held accountable for their actions. Islam has five pillars of Islam, which are the essential religious duties of every adult Muslim who is mentally able. The five pillars are faith, prayer (five times a day), almsgiving, fasting, and pilgrimage. Something related to Islam which is the center of debate these days is Islamic concept of Jihad. Some Muslims consider Jihad as the sixth pillar of Islam. Jihad (struggle) means individual or collective holy war to defend

Muslims and please God. Some people consider Jihad as any sort of effort which can be for helping other Muslims through charity, education, or other means. This idea was mainly emphasized by Khomeini at the early years of Iranian revolution.

Overall, the militant interpretation of Jihad is more correct. Something very important about Jihad is the fact that it should be ordered by the highest leader in the Islamic community. In other words, a person such as Osama bin Laden is in no position to order the Jihad. On the other hand, in Islam there are many different types of leaders; hence, this fact increases the possibility of having someone to do so. According to Islam a person who dies in the Process of Jihad is a martyr. In other words, in Islam the concept of being a martyr and the rewards which a martyr gets is an important subject. A martyr is a person who by his death proves the strength of his beliefs to please others. Moreover, in Islam a martyr is a religious object who serves as a mediator with God. Such a person believes that with his action he will get a reward from God which is direct or free transfer to heaven. Although members of other religions may also believe in this philosophy (cult groups), in Islamic societies a martyr is an individual who sacrifices his life in a struggle against something which he thinks is injustice. For example, those who crashed the planes into the World Trade Center in New York considered themselves as martyrs.

For Muslim people mosques are the most important places for public expression and to pray. In chapter twelve, we discussed about new movement in the Islamic world which is mostly initiated in the mosques. One of the most important mosques for Muslim people is Dome of the Rock in Jerusalem, where Muslims believe from there Muhammad ascended into heaven. Although Jews and Christians also have roots in this building for Muslim it is a very important place and is now one of the main issues in the Israel/Arabs war. Muslims believe in angels, the Day of Judgment, heaven, and hell.

As mentioned before the laws of Islam are many and complex. These laws cover areas such as dietary laws, purity laws, social laws, formal and informal marriage laws, inheritance laws, and commercial transaction laws. These laws are mostly transferred to people through *hadith*. In Islam there are also many cultural rules, which can be interpreted differently by different people. Although in Islam the equality between all humans is a fundamental issue and verbally all Muslim people accept it, but in practice it does not apply to everybody. In today's Islam women do not have equal opportunity compared with men. For example, it is said that women should cover themselves in front of men. We can easily see how this rule is enforced. In several developed Muslim countries there are not restrictions in how women cover themselves. In several Islamic nations only, hair should be covered (use *hejab*). There are yet places which women should wear dark dresses in the hottest places of the world and only their eyes can be seen. Frankly, in the same area men wear white clothes. Finally, the worse condition could be seen in the Taliban Afghanistan in which women were considered nothing or simply as an object. In the Taliban Afghanistan, women not only should cover all their body but also could not even go to school, drive a car, listen to the radio, etc. In addition, in some parts of Islamic nations, in the 21st century, harsh rules such as killing by throwing stones, cutting off hands and head, or slashing victims are enforced. These are examples confirming what was said at the beginning of this chapter: no religion is damaged by its followers as much Islam.

One very important event in the History of Islam is destruction of Islam by Hulagu, grandson of Mongol ruler Genghis Khan in

171

1258. Hulagu led his armies across the Zagros Mountains of Iran and destroyed Baghdad. It is estimated that 1 million Muslims were murdered in this event.

How is the religion in the modern world? Modern world has posed real challenges to traditional religions. Some people in the modern societies believe that religion is neither good nor bad but simply irrelevant. They think religions enforce laws which belong to a thousand years ago. They also think religions are made by highly intelligent and smart people to save their nations and there is no connection between religions and God. These ideas have roots in science. As we discussed in chapter two, there is no connection between spiritual meaning and the existence of the universe. Many people in the modern world think that religions are superstitious thinking for political control. Several religious laws are meaningless. For example, the three major religions believe in a single God but in two of them officially eating pork is prohibited. If for any health reason eating pork is not allowed, why would the same God allow a large portion of his followers to eat it? None of the religion's laws can be explained by science. Nevertheless, despite the appearance of thousands of new ideas and new religious and anti-religious movements around the world in the 20th century, old and main religions not only did not disappear but in many places, they are thriving.

In summary, in this chapter, the main existing religions on earth and their relations with humans were discussed. A brief discussion about different religious ideas was presented. We now know that different nations may have different Gods, something which cannot be explained. If humans are all the same, why do they have different Gods? Or if there is only one God associated with the earth, why do we humans interpret him differently? The same argument is applied to the religions. Why are there so many different religions? Why do those religions which are very close to each other constantly fighting with each other? In this chapter the new ideas about religions were also briefly discussed. In the following chapter, the influence of religions on human behavior and war between nations will be reviewed.

CHAPTER FOURTEEN

Humans and Wars

War is one of the most important natural behaviors of all animals including humans. Fighting between different species or members of one species has been a part of living organisms possibly from the very early stages of evolution. In chapters four and five, the effect of fighting for survival on the evolution of all organisms on earth was discussed. Fighting is actually a natural reaction to a dangerous situation or a response to anger caused by various reasons. During the process of fighting an individual or a group of people either run away from danger or get involved in the war to eliminate the source of anger. Generally, a common way to deal with fear is becoming angry. Therefore, anger is usually associated with underlying fears about something important. Obviously, anger in animals cause several physiological changes that finally lead to performing actions against the source of anger. What can be the source of anger? The source of anger can be any phenomenon, which based on the judgment of the angry individual, is life threatening. We already know that all living organisms need certain and specific things for their survival. Therefore, any factors which are somehow able to imbalance the crucial needs of any organism can cause danger and force the organism to engage in the fight. In previous chapters, in many places it was shown that the most important factors, which are needed for the survival of all animals, are food, territory, and sexual mates. This means that animals usually engage in fighting when their territories, which include food and sexual mate, are in danger. In humans, in addition to the above factors, several other species-specific factors, such as access to energy and need for promotion of ideology, may also be the causative agents of fighting.

During fight, the organisms, which are equipped with better tools, have a better chance to win the fight and destroy the enemies. In animals the tools which are mainly used in the fights are beak, teeth, and claws. It is obvious that physical appearance of an animal, such as body size is also an important factor for a successful fight. Several animal species predict the danger and usually try to trap their enemies before engaging in a fight. They also hide to be safe in case an unpredicted situation takes place. Except several developed monkeys, which may use stones or tree's branches in the fights, the rest of animals usually use their physical and anatomical ability to win a fight. Early humans were acting like their ancestors. They were hiding in caves, using stones, tree's branches and even fire to protect themselves and destroy their enemies. Along with improvement in other aspects of human life, gradually the methods of fighting in humans improved and fighting became more organized and a part of human living. Early humans were fighting mostly with other animals; however, there are indications which show that from early stages in human evolution, *Homo sapiens* could not easily get along with Neanderthals and extinction of Neanderthals may to some degree be due to antagonism between them.

Before discussing about humans and wars we should point out several interesting points. (1) Humans usually do not get involved in fighting with other species except if their actions are directly related to the food or competitions for food sources. (2) Most fights during the history of mankind have been between humans and humans, something which is very rare in other animals. In other words, animals rarely kill the members of their own species but the main reasons for wars between humans have been and still is destroying or killing the members of our own species. (3) Most early wars between humans were for slavery reasons. A population which had more power brought the members of a week population under control and used them as a labor force. (4) Most early wars were related to territorial disputes; therefore, they were mainly between members of neighboring populations. (5) The majority of the wars in recent years were directly related to ideological (especially religions) differences. (6) Although the action of war for any reason is not acceptable, in recent wars humans got more inhuman and got their satisfaction by torturing the enemies, examples, World War II and recent war in Yugoslavia. (7) Recent wars have been between nations which are not even geographically close to each other. (8) Many of the recent wars were initiated for simple reasons. (9) Nearly all wars in the last thousand years were in an organized form; however, recent wars are unusual. For example, a person whose mental situation is not clearly known, with several million dollars lives in a cave and fights with the most powerful nation in the world. (10) Old and conventional weapons are not a factor in the wars any more. The new weapons are chemical or biological, which their use is inhuman. (11) In recent years suicidal missions become new weapons for fighting, one or a small group of people by a suicidal action kills a significant number of innocent people. (12) In recent years armed people do not fight with armed people. It is in fact armed individuals who fight against unarmed individuals. (13) Finally, for the first time we witnessed that a country was dropping bombs in a certain war zone and at the same time, the same country, was dropping food in the same area for the same nation.

A simple review on what was mentioned show that with improvement in the civilizations, fighting between nations got worse and more inhuman. While I was preparing this chapter, I did research on the major human wars and found that the subject of wars in human history is the richest part of our history. There have been over a thousand major wars in our history. I also found that most of the wars in ancient world were between super powers with super powers but in recent years poor nations got engage with super powers mainly because of economic reasons. The major wars in the past have been between super powers in the areas which are now Egypt, China, Persia, Greece and Rome. The recent wars do not follow the same rules. After the September 11 event in the United States, we could see that a group people, who did not accept the existence of 50 per cent (women in Afghanistan) of their own nation, got engaged in a war with the most advanced nation in the whole history of the world.

Since the major focus of this book is on the recent facts that are facing humans, I only did research on the most recent wars and summarized them in the following table. Obviously, the explanation of the details of each one of these wars is not possible and it is out of the limit of this book.

An attempt has been made to only discuss about those conflicts which are the origin of recent problems in the world, something which I think can be easily resolved. What is actually a war? War is a man—made law which involves armed conflict between two or more countries, populations, or nations. It is obvious that the wars are organized by the governments and all members of a nation in the war may not necessarily agree with the war. If a war involves many nations around the world, it is called a world war. A war which is between different members or fractions of one nation is called a civil war. As discussed in the previous chapter, an interesting type of war is the one which is between two nations which follow one religion and both nations claim that their religion is based on love, peace and recognition of human values. The worse possible type of war is the one in which a group of people who follow certain doctrines kill certain segments of their own nations because of a reason which is not acceptable by international laws. Although a rebellion is not by definition a war, I think any action which for any reason ends in killing each other should be considered a war.

Sometimes wars do not directly involve killing but they are only associated with the exchange of words or competition for improvement in armies. In this case the war is referred to as a cold war. Sometimes a war is created in one part of the world and other governments which are not even close to the area benefit from such a war for their own political or economic reasons. It is obvious that termination of these types of wars may cause destruction of a government in another section of the word; therefore, these types of wars are useful only if they exist for a long period of time. The best example of this type of war is the conflict between Arabs and Israel. The only two nations which really suffer from this war and everyday many of them are killed are people who live in the area. A quick review on this conflict show that the two nations involved in the war may be able to resolve their differences, but they cannot do it because continuation of this war is used by certain shaky governments to blame someone or another country and make their own people busy (refer to chapter twelve). Sometimes creation or continuation of a war is useful for economical reason such as increase in employment in factories which make weapons. The worst types of wars are those which are indirectly related to the religious beliefs or racial hate. Examples for these types of wars or fighting are: World War II (Christian/Jews), Northern Island war (Christian/Christians), Middle East war (Jews/Muslims), Iran and Iraq war (Muslims/ Muslims), Pakistan and India war (Muslims and Hindus), Japan and China

(Buddhists/Buddhists), Yugoslavia (Christians/ Muslims/ Christians) and finally the Persian Gulf War (Muslims/ Muslims/ Christians). Needless to mention that, in all of these religions the peace and love in the human communities are the principle of human integrity.

Major wars in the recent history*

a. The 100—year War (1339-1453)
b. The Afghan/Soviet occupation (1979-1989)
c. The Afghanistan (Taliban)/ America War (2001)
d. The American revolution (1775-1783)
e. The Boer War (1880-1881 71889-1902)
f. The Crimean War (1853-1856)
g. The English Civil War (1642-1649)
h. The Falkland War (1982)
i. The French revolution (1789-1799)
j. The Granada Invasion (1983)
k. The India/Pakistan War (1971)
l. The Iranian revolution (1979)
m. The Iran/Iraq War (1980-1988)
n. The Israel/Arabs War (1948—present)
o. The Italy/Ethiopian (1935-1936)

p. The Korean war (1950-1953)

q. The Mexican/American war (1846-1848)

r. The Napoleonic War (1800-1815)

s. The Opium Wars (1839-1860)

t. The Panama/American War (1989)

u. The Persian Gulf War (1991)

v. The Philippine/American War (1899-1902)

w. The Russian Revolution (1917-1921)

x. The seven -year war (1755 -1763)

y. The Spanish Civil war (1936-1939)

z. The United States Civil War (1861-1865)

aa. The Vietnam War (1961-1975)

ab. The World War I (1914-1918)

ac. The World War II (1939 -1945)

ad. Russi and Ukraine war (2022- now)

ae. Iran and Israel war (2025)

* These are major wars. During this period of time, there have been hundreds of other minor wars which are not mentioned.

Of the wars between humans possibly World War II (1939-1945) is the greatest and the most destructive one in recent history. This war was global and covered Europe, Asia, America, and Africa. More than 17 million members of armed forces from different nations were involved in this war and millions of people were killed. A significant number of people killed were those who were not directly involved in the conflict and as we know the followers of a certain religion were killed by torture using the worst inhuman methods. In this war several countries gain economical capabilities and several countries totally collapsed. Also, in this war, chemical and atomic weapons were used. Many kings, leaders, or president were either killed or removed from their power. The events leading to World

War II will not be discussed here, but it is worth it to mention that this war was possibly one of the most shameful actions of human species in history.

The recent war between the United States and Taliban in Afghanistan was possibly the most unusual war. In this war a group of people (Taliban) with ideas that derived from more than one thousand year ago governed on a very poor country and used the most primitive type of rules to promote their ideas. This group overall considered women in the society as an object which were according to them even lower than animals. Nearly all governments in the world knew about the action of such a government and they were not actually doing anything to liberate the real poor people in the area. Obviously, such a government could exist only because someone could financially support it. At the same time a person who did not even have a nationality (Osama bin Laden) found this place a safe base for his hiding site. This person with a limited financial saving and with extremely fanatic ideas promoted certain ideas to several young people and promised a free pass to heaven. Obviously, this group of young people considered the highest possible reward and combined it with their own beliefs and decided to engage in a war with the most powerful country which has ever existed on the surface of the earth. As mentioned above, in this conflict the conventional methods of fighting were not applied. In ordinary wars, usually organized armies face each other and start fighting. This group of people actually wanted to introduce terror in a society and therefore the best target for them was innocent people. We all were witness to the outcome of this action. The action of these people created a new type of war which is now named "war against terrorists".

As mentioned above, in any conflicts using better and more effective weapons in conjunction with an organized army usually led to the victory of the dominant nation or group. Early humans used sharp stones and tree branches to destroy or kill their enemies. With improvement in the knowledge of humans and discovery of metals gradually humans started to make knives and other sharp metal tools such as swords. Obviously, these objects could be used only in close combats and therefore did not have effective use. Later, javelins and archery were developed and gradually with the discovery of explosive chemicals, guns, cannons, mines and bombs were used in wars. Later humans realized that for a better performance in the wars, they should be able to transfer the explosives to distance area, which finally led to making tanks and planes. The low speed of planes made them good targets for enemies; therefore, different sorts of fighters were made. Even the high-speed fighters could not transfer explosives from one part of the world to other sections; therefore, rockets were invented. Gradually more powerful explosive such as atomic bomb and hydrogen bomb and later newer form of weapons such as neutron bombs were made. Although usage of any form of weapons for killing an innocent person is out of the question possibly the worst type of weapons are chemicals and biological weapons. Since the discovery of these weapons many countries found that introduction of poisonous chemicals and biological weapons are really destructive and highly inhuman even by the standard of any wars; therefore, most of the nations in the world condemn the use of chemicals against humans.

As we know, the inhuman behavior of certain people does not have any limits. We were all witness to when in Iran/Iraq war the Iraqi used chemical weapons not only against their enemy (Iran) but also against the people of their own nations. Similarly, the use of biological weapons by the same nation was also under question in

Iran/Iraq and Persian Gulf wars. Regarding the use of biological weapons, we were all witness of such an action in the United States. We saw that an unknown source was mailing letters containing *Bacillus anthracis* to people. The problem associated with the use of biological weapons is not limited to the use of this bacterium which causes anthrax in humans. The real problem can be the introduction of viruses such as Poxvirus variola with the 40% rate of mortality. This virus was eliminated in all nations several years ago but several countries still have access to preserved form of it. As discussed, the subject of this book is the facts which are facing humans. Although using any form of weapons should be prohibited in the world since the use of mass- destruction weapons such as chemical, biological and atomic weapons are inhuman, only these weapons will be briefly discussed here.

Biological and chemical warfare are deadly biological or chemicals agents. Since these weapons can kill a significant number of people, they are called mass—destruction weapons. Chemical weapons are made from highly poisonous or toxic chemical compounds and biological weapons are living microorganisms specifically those which are either resistance to harsh environment (bacterial spores) or those which are highly contagious. Depending on the type of the agent, both chemical and biological weapons cause injury or death when inhaled or have contact with the skin. A chemical or biological attack usually takes place by dispersing the harmful agents into the air. Chemical weapons were first used extensively in World War I (1914-1918) and later in the Iran-Iraq War (1980-1988). As noted above, international agreements prohibit the use of chemical and biological weapons; nevertheless, the number of countries searching for these types of weapons is increasing. Of these countries Iraq is the main one and no international agency or country could so far stop Iraq's actions.

Chemical agents which are usually used as weapons can be grouped in several categories. They may damage the nervous system or cause injury on the skin. Examples of these chemicals are mustard gas, phosgene, chlorine, and hydrogen cyanide. Phosgene causes the lungs to fill with water, chlorine destroys the respiratory tract cells, hydrogen cyanide inhibits oxygen uptake, and mustard gas is a blistering agent which affects skin, eyes, and lungs. The agents affecting nervous system are mainly sarin, soman, tabun, and VX. All these agents can disrupt the normal action of acetylcholine. A small amount of these agents especially VX can cause death within a minute. A number of the chemical agents such as herbicides can cause vegetation death but they are also harmful to humans and animals.

Biological weapons are living organisms; therefore, they are more serious than chemical agents because microorganisms can increase their numbers after release. Biological agents can be bacteria, viruses, or fungi. The best examples for biological weapons are the agents of tularemia, Q fever, yellow fever, smallpox, and anthrax. It is important to mention that the viral infections cannot be cured using what we know as antibiotics. The agent causing the anthrax can be prepared and then introduced in the spore form. Bacterial spores are the most resistant type of living things on the earth. The most effective way for destroying bacterial spores is using high temperature (121 degree C) for at least 20 minutes. Several biological agents are not living microorganisms rather they are the products of microorganisms. Of these, the botulinum toxin which is produced by a bacterium named *Clostridium botulinum,* is the most lethal one and can cause death even with a tiny dose. A gallon of dilute botulinum toxin can poison a city's water system; however, the existing water purification process in many cities can neutralize the toxin. The biological weapons have been used in the past by

Russia, in colonial America by British, by Japan against China, in the United States by the Rajneesh cult in Oregon, and a recent unknown distributor of Anthrax agent in the United States.

One major problem related to the use of chemical and biological agents is the fact that these agents are now in the hand of different groups of people named terrorists and countries do not have any controls on the actions of these groups. These groups used sarin in Japan in the past and anthrax in the United States recently. Nobody knows who has these agents and what types are available to them. In the United States, studies performed in 1950s and 1960s showed that the release of these agents in the large cities can expose millions of people and a terrorist group can do this action with the simplest techniques. Although after release, chemical and biological agents can immediately cause damage in the communities but using masks, antibiotics, and vaccination programs can finally control the effect of these agents. One may ask although the release of biological and chemical agents can be effective on humans but these agents cannot differentiate between enemies and friends. This is true but in practice, the person or the group of people who use these agents protect themselves by using appropriate masks or antibiotics or vaccination programs. One issue associated with the use of mass-destruction weapons is the fact that there are ready to release these agents in suicide attempts.

One of the most devastating weapons of mass destruction is the nuclear bomb. Nuclear bombs have been used against a country only twice, in 1945 by American B-29 bombers during World War II. One major problem associated with an atomic bomb is the fact that this bomb not only produces extensive heat and blast but also releases radioactive substances into the environment. Radiations emitted by radioactive material cause serious problems which finally lead to death. Nuclear bombs can be atomic (fission of atoms) or hydrogen (fusion of two hydrogen atoms). They are simply referred to as A-bombs and H-bombs.

In the A-bomb, high energy neutrons break the atoms of uranium or plutonium and cause release of additional neutrons. As the consequence of this chain-reaction and split of uranium or plutonium atoms, lots of energy equal to several thousand tons of TNT is released. Although purification of uranium or production of enriched plutonium is not a simple task but if by any methods these materials get into the hands of people with some basic scientific knowledge, they may be able to use them.

In the 1950s, the H-bomb was developed. In an H-bomb, massive energy (several hundred times more than the A-bomb) is released after fusion of hydrogen atoms, what take place on the surface of the sun (refer to chapter 2). The problem associated with the nuclear weapons is the fact that they can be carried by a small plane and can be charged relatively by a simple method. The neutron bomb has deadly effect on living organisms including humans but does not damage buildings. The neutron bomb and H-bomb cannot be easily used.

Above data show a number of facts which present humans are facing. I think international agencies should somehow control these weapons. The reason why countries are searching for atomic bombs is the intense competition between nations. I think humans should not wait for something to happen and then search for the cure.

The weapon of any kind produced by different nations should be used by certain populations against other populations in wars. In each nation certain people which are overall referred to as an

army use these weapons in wars. An army is a disciplined group of people trained for wars. Discussing about army is not a part of this book's subject but it should be pointed out that nearly in all countries around the world a significant amount of the total incomes of the countries are used for preparation of weapons and training the army personnel. There are governments in the world that do not feed their nations but use their income for their military system, which finally means the maintenance and stability of their governments. The composition of armies has changed in many ways during the history of mankind starting from civilizations in the Tigris-Euphrates Valley and the Nile. At present the United States has the most advanced and prepared military in the whole world and a significant amount of the country's income is used in military services. At present, production of warfare is one of the busiest and the most beneficial businesses for a number of nations in the world. To present a fact, it should be noted that each minute 500,000 dollars are spent on weapons in the world which will be 262,800,000,000 dollars annually. Can we imagine how this amount could be used for improvement of human lives?

This chapter present the facts associated with wars. Since the final message of this book are suggestions for corrective actions in the human communities, briefly the effect of one of ongoing wars, which caused recent major problems in the world, will be discussed. This war is the one which started between Israel and Arabs (Jews and Muslims) in 1948 over the historic land of Palestine. As discussed before, Palestine is a land that all three major religions have roots in it. Although, since 1979 several peace treaties related to this war has been signed but the conflict is still in progress and gets worse day by day. As discussed in chapter five, one of the major places, which were inhabited by early *Homo sapiens* several thousand years ago, is a place which is now Israel, this means that the people who were living in these areas were very close and if we do molecular analysis of the genetic materials in the people in this area, we will see lots of genetic relations. These people started to segregate socially after appearance of Judaism and later with complete segregation due to the appearance of Islam. Throughout the history, the Palestine has been many times conquered by different invaders. In the AD 135 Jewish people settled in this place and considered it their home. In the 1890s, Theodor Herzl suggested the establishment of a Jewish state in the Palestine; however, at the time a part of this area was the home of Arabs and most of them were Muslims. Gradually, these two nations settled in this area and lived with each other normally and without any major problems. Later, Jews from other parts of the world, especially Europe, moved to this area.

At the time, this area was ruled by Ottoman Empire and since people were neglected by the ruler, poverty, diseases, and malnutrition affected the people. It is important to mention that this area has lots of strategic, political and economic values because of its location and its distance to the Suez Canal. Due to anti-Jewish movement in Europe in the early 20th century, gradually Jewish immigrated to this area and their population increased. The people (Arabs and Jews) were living close to each other and doing trade between them including the Jews buying land from the Arabs. This caused the expansion of Jewish lands. Up to this point still these people could peacefully live side by side. The conflict started when Jews started to establish a homeland for themselves. During World War I the Ottoman Empire was defeated and the control of the area shifted to the British.

The British promised equal opportunity to both Arabs and Jews but could not predict what might happen. Later, in 1922, Palestine was divided into two parts of east and west and this was the spark between the two nations. Gradually, Jews and Arabs started attacking each other and a new war started. After World War II, because millions of Jews were killed in Europe, the western countries agreed with a Jewish state. Arabs started to resist the idea but in 1947 the United Nations (UN) passed resolution dividing Palestine into two Jewish and Arab states. The action of UN was accepted by Jews but not Arabs and finally in 1948 Israel was established. Arabs around the world oppose this action and since this date there have been many different types of conflicts between the same people who were living very friendly side by side for many years. So far, hundreds of people from both sides are killed in different conflicts. As discussed before, this area is very important strategically. This means that countries such as the United States like this area to be stable and at the same time friendly toward the United States. Arabs consider the action of the United States as an open support of Israel. On the other hand, a number of countries in this area which have lots of internal problems and their governments are shaky, like to see an active and ongoing situation to refer to and make their people busy. Those who really suffer are the people who are really living in this area.

As we already know, since religion is a very sensitive subject, those who want to gain from this conflict gradually changed the title of the conflict between these two nations to Jews/Arabs war and made it even worse. Recently, they are trying to even change it to conflict between Muslim and Christians. This war is now the main cause of many problems around the world and many countries, agencies and even the ordinary people in the area tried to solve the issue but could not. I think this conflict can be easily resolved if the leaders of both nations decide to do so. How come two groups of people with two different religions cannot live side by side? Since a part of this area is important to all three major religions, maybe establishing a green zone which does not belong to anybody but

God can resolve the situation. What is important for humanity is the fact that people in this area die for nothing except insist on their religious beliefs. History showed that this war, similar to all other wars will eventually end. Is not it better to stop it now? Is not it better to predict occurrence of similar conflict in the future and prevent it now? In chapter seventeen this subject will be discussed.

In this chapter the natural behavior of humans toward fighting was discussed. It was shown that the conflicts between nations in the past have been mainly associated with access to food and holding territories. In the recent years, new issues such as access to energy and insist on religious beliefs became the new tools justifying the wars between the nations. The subjects of weapons and how all nations use most of their incomes to prepare themselves for killing other humans were also discussed. We now know that a number of man-made weapons are actually very easy to make and can be introduced in the societies very easily. We now know that the wars between humans entered a new phase. People are afraid to be exposed to an infectious agent which has been eliminated everywhere after many efforts. People cannot normally go to work. People are anxious and expect things which cannot be predicted. In this chapter, the major wars in the recent history of mankind were mentioned and one of the major ones, which is the center of recent problems in the world, was discussed.

CHAPTER FIFTEEN

Human and Science/Technology

It is all because of improvements and increases in the scientific knowledge of human beings that put them in the position where they are now. Since early stages of human evolution, they started to make simple tools and gradually discovered and invented new things. Humans are now in a stage, which has plan for travel in space. In spite of huge advancements in human technology, the distribution of average scientific knowledge among people on earth is not the same around the world. At the same time that we witness progress in science and technology in countries such as the United States we also see countries which are not able to make or manufacture a small screw. This statement does not imply that certain nations are more intelligent or smarter. It simply shows how an organized population can solve its problems much better than an unorganized nation.

In a country such as the United States, even a first-grade student is engaged in scientific experiments. In contrast, there are now places in the world where students read only one subject (religious book) nearly all day every day. Interestingly, the book is not even in their own native languages and the students should memorize the whole book. According to general rules, these students are in an education program but the application of their education for their own society or other societies is not clear. The issue becomes more interesting when we know that these students do not have any choice and therefore should only follow what their parents want them to do. A first-grade student in the United States has the same capacity and brain as a student in an undeveloped county. It is only the society which forms the future of these two students. In the United States the government is supporting education and helps scientists to prepare humans for travel to Mars but in a country like the Taliban's Afghanistan people were not even allowed to fly even a paper kite. These facts show the gap between different countries and prove the dependency of certain nations on advanced technology from other nations. To me this fact is very important in the relations between nations and therefore is one of the major problems which humans are facing now. In this chapter, we briefly discuss about the scientific improvement of humans and the application of these improvements for better living in the future.

What is science? Pure science is finding a systematized knowledge and the ability to prove it by veritable sense experience. Application of scientific knowledge and search for its practical use is named technology. As mentioned above, humans have been searching and trying to discover new things from early history. In fact, painting on the wall of caves can be considered some sort of experiment by early humans. Astronomical observation, use of simple tools, preparation of metal tools, ability to distinguish between disease and healthy states, and use of different chemicals are examples of early human scientific works. Historical records show that Babylonians had improved mathematical knowledge and Egyptians could treat certain diseases. Greeks were possibly the first people who searched for fundamental causes of natural phenomena and practically worked on the scientific investigations. After the death of Alexander, the Great, many new ideas in the field of astronomy, botany, and medicine were presented in Greece. New discoveries, especially in astronomy, were done by Romans during the Middle Age. Many nations including Greek, Chinese, and Arabs significantly contributed to science. A number of Chinese innovations such as manufacturing of paper, production of gunpowder, and use of printing and compass had significant impact on the progress of Europe. Around the 9th century Baghdad become the center of scientific works and gradually scientific knowledge was transferred to Europe through Spain and Sicily. In Europe scientific centers were established and many advanced discoveries in astronomy were made by Galileo, Kepler and later Copernicus. In the 17th century modern scientific methods were used in science and Galileo introduced advance scientific instruments such as the telescope. Gradually, the microscope, barometer, pendulum clock and thermometer were used in scientific experiments and in 1687 Isaac Newton presented the universal law of gravitation. The work of English, German, and French scientists led to new discoveries in physics, mathematics, biology, and chemistry. In the 18th century, the atomic theory of matter was presented by Dalton; the electromagnetic theories were introduced by Faraday and Maxwell; and the law of the conservation of energy was enunciated by Joule. The most controversial biological theory, evolution, was put forward by Darwin (Chapters four and five) in1859. New findings such as quantum theory and relativity took place in the 20th century. Increase in communications between scientists and improvements in the publications had significant impact on development of sciences.

National and international scientific organizations were established and governments got involved in the improvement of scientific knowledge by supporting the scientists and establishing patent offices. Most advanced discoveries in pure sciences, especially in the fields of medicine, biology, and chemistry took place in late 20th century. Along with the improvement in the pure sciences, technology was also developed significantly. Science is in fact the understanding of eternal laws of nature but it is the use of scientific findings and practical manifestations of technology which changed the world in recent years.

This is one of the main reasons that the gaps between different nations got wider and many new unknown problems raised in the human societies these years. In developed countries, gradually simple tools were changed to more complex ones and changed human lives. Although many early technological findings were done by the early humans in Africa and later in Asia, the modern technology is now only in western countries. At present, the majority of third world countries do not have even the basic knowledge about technology. Although there are countries, which can adapt technology to their societies they are also dependent on countries with advanced technology. For example, there are countries in which cars and televisions are assembled but the main parts of these products are not manufactured by themselves. They only have the knowledge to put the parts together. What does this mean? It means that at present most of the world population depends on a minority group of nations which are advanced in technology.

The earliest human artifacts such as sharp stones were made by the early humans in Africa about 2.3 million years ago. The actual tool making started with the use of fire about 40,000 years ago. Although a small number of animals have the ability to use tools but the capacity of tools' making and creating artifacts is only a human task. This is in fact one of the most important abilities of humans and possibly the main reason which humans significantly differ from animals.

Gradual improvement in the human knowledge affected all different aspects of human lives during history. Humans learned to use fire, prepare cloth, make clay utensils, and wooden baskets. Gradually, metal such as copper were used for making objects such as jewelry. In about 3000 BC humans started to make and use Bronze and tools made of Bronze were used in agriculture. Making two-wheeled carts and using them for transportation can be considered another important finding of humans.

The beginning of engineering is indeed associated with building the pyramid in Egypt about 2600 BC. The rise of military led to making and manufacturing helmets, bows, spears, shields, and swords, which was followed by making chariots in Egypt and Persia. The first networking and road systems were introduced by Persians and later extended to the Mediterranean area. After destruction of the Persian Empire by Alexander the Great, the shipbuilding by Greeks affected the wars and trades in the area. The Roman engineers improved making the buildings, sewers, sports arenas and bridges. From 500 AD to 1500 great technological advancements were made in the agriculture and transportation by Greeks, Romans, Chinese and Islamic cultures.

Inventions of clock and the printing press had major influences on human life. The Gutenberg printing discovery affected the rapid spread of knowledge and gradually all people got access to printed texts. By the end of the Middle Ages, the technological progress was transferred to Western Europe and cities such as London, Amsterdam and Paris became the center of new technology. Although all discoveries up to the17th century were considered important for human improvements, it was the industrial revolution in England which changed the world. Different sorts of factories were established in this country around 1740. Of all improvements in this period possibly the most important one is the development of the steam engine in England and the United States. Gradually, the pace of innovation was transferred to the United States by new immigrants.

The telegraph connected most major cities to each other and finally at the end of the 19th century Thomas Edison introduced the light bulb which led to the use of generating electric power for lighting. Inventions of telephone, phonograph, radio, motion picture, automobile, and airplanes completed most previous inventions. Thousands of household appliances, and skyscrapers were made by humans and gradually technology became a real fact of everyday ordinary life. In the 20th century the United States became the technological leader in the world and by highly organized programs a great nation was born. Since then, nearly all major technological improvements are made in the United States. Development of computers and transistors revolutionized the world and thousands of new things were invented.

Space programs and communication created new environments in the world. The movies made in the United States showing the American type of living were released to all different parts of the world. With the help of television and radio programs people around the world became familiar with things which they could not believe. For example, there are still places in the world where the bride and groom do not see each other before the wedding day but the people in the same area could see sexual relation between young people in the United States. In several Islamic countries women cannot even show their faces but the same women could see American beaches on television. This created some sort of silent social revolution in a number of these societies which are under too much pressure by their governments. Some sociologists suggest that recent anti-American movements in a number of these countries may be related to envy in these societies.

Even in several western countries, people think that advanced technologies in the United States is threatening the quality of life in the world. Supporters of this viewpoint think that the earth's resources are limited and that human life must be structured around a commitment to control the growth of industry and the use of energy. In contrast, there are people who think that modern societies will continue to grow as they are and changes in the societies cannot and should not be controlled. At present all nations in the world for some sort of technological reasons depend on the United States. The population of the United States is about 5 per cent of the whole world population but they possess 60 per cent of the entire world's wealth. Most of this wealth belongs to a small number of the population in the United States who are all men.

In this chapter the importance of science and technology in the development and progress of human beings were discussed. It was shown how the early inventions and scientific findings were transferred from Asian countries to Europe and then gradually spread into the United States. We **now know** that the technological gaps between the United States and the majority of countries around the world are huge and are getting wider day by day. We also know that it is impossible to slow down the technological improvements in the United States. I think humans should not expect the United States to slow down its progress. In fact, other countries should learn from the United States and try to get closer to this country by effective planning programs. Although in all countries, including the United States, major positions are in the hands of men but this imbalance proportion is out of the question in certain places. In a significant number of countries around the world nearly 50 per cent of the whole population (all women) is second hand citizens. They should use the power and ability of all citizens and build their nations. In addition, third world countries should educate their people in a correct way. Reading a text does not necessarily mean that a person is educated. People should have opportunity to learn the right things in free societies.

CHAPTER SIXTEEN

Human and Space Travel

One may ask, since we are having so many problems on the surface of the earth why would humans even think about traveling into space. Some people say the cost associated with space programs should be used for feeding people on earth. I think there are other easier ways which humans can help each other and stop starvation in the world. Stopping the space program and using its cost for other reasons on earth should be the last choice. The reasons why humans think about space travel are: (1) Humans cannot stop improvement in their scientific progress. The vast imaginations of humans are endless and out of control. (2) With the speed at which humans are using resources on the earth, in the future they may need to have access to some sort of valuable chemicals at least on planets which are close to the earth. (3) I think the most important discovery of mankind throughout its history on the surface of earth is proving the existence of other different or similar types of life somewhere in space. (4) As discussed before, there is a possibility that life on the earth originated by some sort of life which reached the earth in the past from other places. If this can be a possibility, we should also be able to transfer our life to other planets. Now the question is, can we really travel to other planets and if we can how far can we go? We also want to know whether other intelligent forms of life have come and visit us in the past. Did UFOs visit us and are they real?

Since ancient times, humans have dreamed about leaving earth and exploring other worlds. This dream became reality first in 1957 and then 1961 when humans started to explore space. Since then, astronauts have ventured into space on many occasions and even lived there for several months. The moon has been visited by man and mankind walked on the moon. Robotic explorers have journeyed even further than the moon and visited other parts of the solar system. New instruments and spacecrafts were used to study solar system, the Milky Way galaxy, and the universe. After preliminary exploration, space stations were made and the space shuttle is used for exploration and safe return to the earth.

In previous chapters we discussed the beliefs (in nearly all religions) associated with the existence of heaven out of earth boundaries and transfer of soul to heaven. Although this idea does not have any scientific support it at least proves how humans are interested to learn more about space and what is in space. Although several countries, especially Russia, contributed to many discoveries related to the space program most of the explorations and interesting findings up to date are the results of the efforts of the American scientists and engineers, another technological superiority which contribute to the gap between the United States and the rest of the world. Traveling into space is not an easy task. Even for a simple mission thousands of different factors should be extensively studied and evaluated before starting the project. For those missions in which astronauts should guide the spacecraft and their presence in the spacecraft during the mission is essential, the number of factors which should be seriously evaluated before flight is even higher. For the missions which may last several months, years or in future centuries, the problems become more complex and sometimes in reality impossible. Below, only a small number of major scientific factors which directly influence a space mission will be briefly discussed.

As discussed in chapter two, space is a vast and a harsh environment for humans and man-made instruments. Radiations from the sun and other cosmic sources can weaken materials and harm the human body extensively. The radiations are especially tense in an area around the earth named the Van Allen belts. In the vacuum condition, any object becomes very hot when directly exposed to the sun and extremely cold when in the shadow of the earth or another planet. This means that the first issue related to travel to space is the design of a spacecraft that can withstand extreme conditions in space. Design and preparation of such a spacecraft is costly and if we add the cost of other related issues to this, for a simple mission several hundred million and for a more complicated one several hundred billion or trillion dollars are needed. This is one of the main reasons that only the United States can afford simple missions. The second most important need for traveling to space is energy source. Energy is required for launch (neutralizing gravity), speed, return and operation of electrical instruments during the mission. The energy capacity of the energy source used in the mission should be at maximum level and its volume should be in the minimum range in any space program. In space, fuels such as ordinary gas cannot be used. The energy source should be those which do not need oxygen to burn. For short missions, liquid fuels which do not need oxygen and for long mission atomic fuel can be used. For missions close to the earth, sun's energy can be used to charge batteries in the spacecrafts. The third most important factor needed for the space traveling is training extremely healthy, young, and knowledgeable astronauts.

The astronauts should be medically suitable for the programs and should have general knowledge about nearly all scientific subjects. Finding suitable individuals and later training them is very hard, costly and time consuming. Human cannot stay in space for a long time and for long- distance traveling, short- time age of a normal person is not sufficient. When a spacecraft with one or more astronauts leave the earth, immediately additional factors such as access to oxygen, medical services, water, and food become major issues. Likewise, method for disposal or recycling astronauts' waste becomes an issue. For long-term travel, exercise equipment, a comfortable sleeping area, clean bathroom, shower, etc, will be added to the existing issues. In addition to the above basic problems, there are many other issues which limit the travel of humans to relatively far areas of space. One of the most important factors associated with long-term travel in space is the distance between planets, solar systems, and galaxies. As discussed in chapter two, these distances are huge and unbelievable. For example, imagine a spacecraft is planning to go to the closest solar system (refer to chapter two), which is about four light—years away from us. Imagine that this solar system has a planetary system and one of its planets is like earth. The distance of this planet to earth will be about 40,000,000,000,000 kilometers. Now, imagine the spacecraft take three days to travel 300,000 kilometers (the time which took Apollo 11 to travel from earth to the moon). Such a spacecraft should travel for 1,000,000 years to reach this solar system. Now, compare the average life expectancy of human beings which is around 50 -60 years with the time which is needed to reach the first solar system. If this imaginary spacecraft carries only three astronauts, imagine how much extra material should be carried with them. This example shows that by a normal method of traveling in space, it is 100 percent impossible to send a person to even the first solar system. Then, what can be done? This problem can be solved by either increasing the speed of the spacecraft or putting the astronauts in a sleep or combination of both. Even if we send a spacecraft to the first solar system with the speed of light (or close to the speed of light), still the spacecraft needs four years to reach the target.

Scientists are completing studies on aging and methods to put humans to sleep for many years and then wake them up whenever they need. However, this is somehow like fiction, but humans may solve this issue in the future. At present we can keep the microorganisms in the liquid nitrogen for many years and bring them to life whenever we want. This procedure may be also applied to humans in the future.

Now imagine that a normal person finally reaches the first solar system and lands on a planet like earth. The first report sent by this person takes four years to reach to earth. Obviously, he will receive the response to his first report four years later. This means that a one—hour conversation will take several hundred years to complete. Needless to mention that if this imaginary astronaut is still healthy and alive, his/her knowledge, based on the earth standard, is out dated. The example given above was an imaginary travel to space.

We know that the chance that we win find a planet in the first and the closest solar system is very low. Now imagine if we decide to travel to the solar systems in the radius of 100 light years to finally find a planet with some sort of life. Likewise, travel to a radius of 1,000-10,000 light years to find an intelligent form of life is impossible. If we add all other issues related to travel to space, such as, zero gravity problems, navigation in space, correct flight paths, contact with the earth, movement of the target, crew support, etc. We reach the point that it is almost impossible to find or reach another civilization with existing "human" abilities. Maybe in thousands of years we will become able to solve many unknown problems and finally find a planet suitable for living in other solar system. This dream may become a reality if we are at least able to send the human DNA molecules to other places and then be able to convert the DNA to a complete living human; however, this is more like a science fiction story. All above information shows that we cannot easily explore different parts of even our own galaxy to find intelligent life. It also means that other intelligent lives have more or less the same problems which we have. In other words, the UFO and especially those which carry human-like creatures to earth are not likely to be true. Even if we assume that UFOs without astronauts visited the earth before, nobody can really explain why these UFOs spend so much time to reach the earth and finally, they only showed themselves to a small group of earthy people and left us? Those who believe in UFOs argue and say that human knowledge is not at the level to understand UFOs. This cannot be acceptable because if we can see the UFOs, it means they have some sort of physical appearance. Many of physical laws in the universe are the same, so the UFOs should also follow the same laws.

Nevertheless, the universe is full of mysteries, and the most important one is the existence of the universe itself. There are other forms of life in the universe. The question is: can we reach them or they reach us? Although humans may not be able to travel into space soon, we can at least explore the planets in our own solar system for the existence of life.

Out of all nine planets in our solar system, Mars is a planet which might have and still have some sort of microorganisms. Although nearly all planets in our solar system have been visited by man—made spacecrafts but none of them except Mars can harbor life. In our solar system, the only planet which overall has the closest condition to earth is Mars. So far, several unmanned missions to Mars have been fulfilled. Scientists collected lots of data and there is a possibility that in the next 20 years humans may land on the surface of Mars. This planet is only 20 minutes of light- years (360,000,000 kilometers) away from us and its distance to us is not even comparable with the planets in other solar systems or galaxies.

In this chapter the possibility of space travels was briefly discussed. By simple calculations and explanations, we could show that space travels are very costly and those which involve long distances are nearly impossible if we consider the present humans' knowledge. By the same token, other forms of intelligent life also cannot reach us easily due to the extreme distance between objects in the universe. In short term, humans may only be able to travel to Mars which has the closest conditions to earth. This planet may have some sort of primitive life.

The main objective of presenting this chapter was to show that we cannot easily travel away from earth. Even if in the future technology allows us to travel to other planets, the consequence of such travel will only be useful for scientific enjoyment and would not have any real travel value. If astronauts travel to deep space they may not be able to come back. Even if the astronauts accept to leave earth forever and start a one-way journey, how many of them can actually go there? They only can take our genetic materials to other places which would not have any value for those who are living on earth. These facts show that at least for now all humans are bound to earth and they cannot escape from it. They need the same air, the same water and the same soil. Although our bodies are made of the same materials, atoms and molecules in our bodies are so organized that makes us living things. Each human is a unit of biology with vast power of thinking capacity but limited physical ability. We know that we are from this planet and will finally end forever on this planet. We never go anywhere and never come back in any form. Therefore, why do not we use our lives and the facilities on this planet properly and live in peace in our short lives? In the following pages, the relation between us and the earth, and the facts associated with our lives on earth, and suggestions for better living will be discussed.

CHAPTER SEVENTEEN

Conclusion

In previous chapters, attempts were made to give an overall review of *Homo sapiens,* their origin, activities, relations with each other and environment, and their future. We now know that each human being is a unit of a living organism with specific characteristics. The appearance at birth of each human on the surface of earth is not under his/her own control and similarly the disappearance or death is also uncontrollable. During the history of mankind, never have two individuals with similar characters existed. Everyone is unique both genetically and in the way he/she thinks. The human species differ from the rest of the living world on the surface of the earth mostly because of its higher intelligence. This species lives on a planet, which compare to the grandeur of the universe, is only a tiny object in the corner of the Milky Way galaxy. Since the creator of the universe and the reason for its existence is not clear, obviously the existence of humans, which are only a small part of this system, is even more questionable. We do not know exactly if only our planet harbors life or if there are other places which have some sort of living organisms. We do not even know why out of over two million different species on the surface of the earth only human has a limited knowledge about their positions in the universe. What we do know for sure know is the fact that the existence of human beings on the surface of the earth is relatively a new phenomenon in the history of the earth and obviously the universe. We also know that humans are the outcome of many evolutionary changes which took place in living organisms in the past. Close biological similarities between other organisms, especially animals, with humans, show that we are a part of life on the earth. We are not distinctive or a special form of living created in several days on the surface of the earth by a power which its existence is also under question.

Scientific findings show that, humans from their early appearance were behaving like their ancestors and were constantly in the fight for living. Gradually and during history, humans accumulated knowledge, found better ways to live and started to become civilized. Increased in population and therefore need for organization led to the establishment of communities around the world. Obviously, throughout history different communities faced different problems and found various ways for better living and each community established new customs in its territory.

Along with the increase in the number of individuals in the population, simple forms of laws and rules were established and in each community a group of individuals enforced the laws and tried to organize the societies. Since the early days humans were curious about themselves and the environment around them, gradually in the most populated parts of the world highly intelligent individuals raised and tried to control the communities and enforce better and more meaningful ideas. Obviously, these individuals were successful because they introduced themselves as the bridges between the creator and the people.

For primitive humans who could not be controlled easily, the existence of some sort of rewards or punishment could help the leaders to have better control of the communities. Mystery of life for early humans, in conjunction with the promise of leaders led to the appearance of early religions. Early religions came one by one and for better success, each one connected itself to the previous one. The new leaders claimed that they had authorities to complete the previous ideas and their thought is the final one. As we know, during the human history, thousands of new ideas and new religions were introduced and most of them either disappeared or could absorb only a small number of followers. Of these religions a number of the major ones ruled on the surface of the earth for several hundred years and enforced their ideas to their communities in different ways. In the history of mankind in many instances there has been unfair judgments enforced by religious beliefs, of which possibly the trail of Socrates (469-339 BC) and Galileo (1564-1642) are the most famous recorded ones. Socrates, the Greek philosopher was regarded with suspicion toward the established religion of the time. He was charged in 399 BC with neglecting the gods and corrupting the morals of the young people. As we know, his ideas were condemned and he was sentenced to die. He himself fulfilled the execution by drinking a cup of hemlock. Galileo's story at least had a better ending. Galileo, an Italian physicist and astronomer, was convicted and was sentenced to life imprisonment by the Roman Catholics because of his revolutionary and at the same time controversial ideas about astronomy. Doubtless, Galileo was a great scientist and nobody knows what he could do for humans if he was free to present his great scientific ideas.

Throughout history, increase in the scientific knowledge gradually limited the power of religions in societies and different religious ideas one by one faced the strong scientific oppositions and were eliminated. These processes did not necessarily reject the religions by scientists of the time. After appearance of Islam, many scientific findings were presented by scientists in the Islamic world. These scientists believed in Islam but were still contributing in the advancement of science.

As discussed in the previous chapters, improvement in science and technology in the last 200 years gradually limited the influence of religions in the communities and young people started to believe in the realities, something which was not acceptable by many religious leaders. As discussed before, of the main religions in the world, Islam has the most laws and rules. In Islam it is believed that a religious leader can actually govern the society. We were witness of such an idea in 1979 when Khomeini established an Islamic country in the Middle East. He actually wanted to enforce the Islamic laws and export his Islamic ideas to other countries. Soon he and his followers realized that the 20th century world cannot be governed by the rules and laws established over a thousand years ago. As an example, in Islam the interest of money is not allowed and both those who pay the interest and the ones who receive it are involved in sins. We know that the banking system and economy are based on interest. How can a system continue its existence in the 20th century if that system does not follow the basic rules of the economy? Obviously, the religious leaders in this country somehow ignored this basic law of Islam and, as we now know, at present they are only enforcing simple and sometimes meaningless rules of Islam, such as limits of freedom for women. We were also witness to another type of extreme religious ruler, Taliban, in Afghanistan. Although the Taliban is history and at present other religious governments do not have any real power, but we should not forget that these types of movements will not disappear forever except an intelligent action is enforced by international agencies. We should not forget that capturing a cave man will not solve all problems which humans are facing now. Soon, new types of issues will be introduced in civilized communities.

Advancement in knowledge and increase in the world populations, as well as new scientific findings and improvements in technology; especially during the last two hundred years, led to establishment of better forms of living dominantly in the western part of the world. Increased population forced people to search and try to find more productive methods for agriculture and transportation. Both these processes needed a relatively cheap source and easily available source of energy. The discovery of crude oil and its use in nearly all aspects of human life is possibly one the main reasons which led to many discoveries and improvements in technology. As we know, simple technology was first moved from the east to Europe and then nearly entirely to the United States. The whole technology and industries became dependent on the cheap energy. Although western countries had access to their own limited source of oil, the majority of oil reserves were discovered in the Middle Eastern countries. Obviously, for better and safe access to the energy source, western countries tried to have reliable friends in the oil- rich areas. As discussed before, most of the oil- rich countries do not have advanced technology for discovery and actual use of their crude oil, meaning both buyers and sellers depend on each other. Obviously, any imbalance situation in the oil flow, such as the Iranian revolution and Persian Gulf War created major panics in the economy of the western countries. As discussed before, corrupted governments, religious beliefs and especially the technological lags forced people in oil- rich countries to search for a solution. Nearly all major countries in the oil- rich countries have governments which are not popular between their own people. Most of these countries are also followers of Islam, which according to their beliefs is a revolutionary and advanced religion. A major ongoing situation in the world—Jews and Arabs war- also became an extra and useful reason for people in the area to struggle for freedom. People in these areas used these issues to express their feelings. As we learned in the previous chapters, in many countries around the world human rights and freedom, comparable to the standards in the western countries, do not exist. People in a number of these countries are constantly under pressure and nearly all aspects of their lives, such as what they wear, what they eat, what they listen to, what they write, and what they watch on the television are under the control of their governments. With improvement in communications and increase in the knowledge of people, too much pressure caused appearances of many different types of Islamic movements in the area. New types of wars and struggles started in history of mankind. Young people who did not have any choices and were trained by religious groups became ready to kill themselves and many other innocent people to express their feelings. We were all witness of what has happened on Sept. 11, 2001. As discussed before, nobody is born as a terrorist; it is only uncontrolled environments which create criminals. Those who think this sort of movement will end soon are wrong. These actions can be eliminated only after their sources are found and destroyed. What can we expect from a young child who spends nearly all his childhood life memorizing religious books? Obviously, a child who can memorize a book (which is not even in his native language) has the ability and potential to become a good physician and help its own community. Who is responsible for such an ongoing and dangerous situation in the world? I think these children are victims and international agencies should save them.

The intense activities of humans, which directly relate to increase the uncontrolled population of humans, caused many more drastic changes in the world. Uncontrolled use of fossil energy gradually damaged the quality of air, and green areas in the world. Bad quality of air resulted in the appearance of new forms of diseases. Industrial activities damaged drinking water in many parts of the world. The oil, which has been formed during the last one hundred million years, will be consumed by humans in only a few more years and lots of waste material will replace the oil around the world. Human activities not only put the human life in danger but also drastically affected other forms of lives on earth. Many species disappeared. According to the United Nations' reports, nearly 1.5 billion humans are considered poor. Out of these people one third of them do not have enough food to eat. Each year a significant number of poor people are added to the world population. Each year about fourteen million individuals die before age five.

Nearly one fourth of the world population is illiterate and a significant number of educated ones can only read or write which does not necessarily mean understanding the realities. Unfortunately, the illiterates are the best targets for the opportunists. There are still traces of racisms in the world. Women which are 52 percent of the world populations are still under pressure and in some countries are absolutely considered second hand citizens.

The gaps between societies are getting wider every day. In several countries homosexuals can marry but in some places in the world they are executed because of their actions. In some community's sexual relation is a part of freedom but in several societies the relation between different sexes is under the control of the leaders. In western world, people can express their ideas easily but in several countries even watching western television is not allowed. New diseases such as AIDS may sweep off the entire population of several countries in Africa.

Just now while I am writing in this world, there is a leader who would not mind to destroy the whole world population including his own people by the use of chemical and other forms of mass destruction. None of the international agencies do any action to correct these problems. During the last six years many people around the world tried to convince international communities about the life of women in Afghanistan but nobody cared. The world attention about Afghan people became a subject only after the event which caused the death of several thousand innocent people in a terrorist action. Is not it better to solve the problems before the consequences of the problems damage our societies? At any given time, there is a major ongoing war on the surface of the earth and people are now thinking about the possible need for war against diseases which were eliminated several years ago. People are afraid to fly. Overall, humanity is in its lowest possible level. People are afraid to work in tall buildings and simply nobody can predict what will happen to him/her when they leave their homes in the morning.

The above facts show that *Homo sapiens* are trying to destroy its own species along with other things on earth. There is no doubt that human problems get even worse in the future. The world simply became like a jungle. What can be done before it is too late? There is no doubt that any action should be taken by international agencies in the shortest possible time. It is shown that whenever all countries around the world decided to do a positive action, they could fulfill it. The best example is the eradication of smallpox, which was done by WHO and supports of all countries.

How can we solve all existing problems which are facing mankind now? To answer this question, we should first review history. In previous chapters the human's behaviors and overall history of mankind with all different types of wars between nations were discussed. If we review our history, we will see that in the past nearly all super powers, such as Persian, Egyptian, Arabs, Chinese, Mongolian, Greek, and Roman, while in power, destroyed their enemies to expand their territories. In nearly all wars that took place in the past there has not been any kindness. The leaders of super powers did their best to destroy the defeated nations. One may say the same rules should be applied in the world now. Super powers should wipe out the nations which do not follow the accepted international laws. We know that, at present super powers have such abilities? Can super powers do whatever they want? The answer is, no. We know that the world in the 21st century is not like what it was thousands of years ago. We see that a superpower not only cannot destroy a nation, which is in the war, but also sends millions of tons of food to the same nation. Although there are tensions all around the world, no nation can simply destroy another nation by similar rules applied in the past. All these facts show many existing issues are slowly damaging humanity. Of course, a number of humans' behaviors cannot be changed overnight. For example, nobody can change religious beliefs of people who throughout their lives believed in some religious rules. I think nobody should even try to do so. What the humans in the 21st century can do is prevent the source of problems and try to control them. Humans should search for a method to provide equal opportunity for all children around the world and let them have access to the right form of education. There are many children in Africa and Asia who can be astronauts, engineers, physicians, scientists, etc., but they never get a chance to go to school. They do not have access to opportunities because of their environments. There are countries in which a significant number of the population does not receive enough food, but their leaders spent most of the countries' incomes for their personal use or buying weapons to engage in wars with their neighbors.

I think human beings will finally decide to search and find a solution to confront with existing problems. I also think we will finally reach a conclusion that the world should become only one country. The borders should not separate people and all these present countries should become the states of an international government. The international government should have absolute power to immediately neutralize any inhuman actions in the world. The actions of religious leaders should be controlled and people should be allowed to practice the love and peace parts of religions. The wrong interpretation of religious beliefs which force humans to kills each other should be stopped. We all know that all religions were first established for guidance of people and all of them claim that they are enforcing God's law. Nobody can believe that God enjoys the action of a group people who crash planes into buildings. The international communities should stop these actions from their onsets. The international government should protect children and not let opportunists train them for destruction. Obviously, an international government can do its job properly only if all existing countries support its establishment. The act of war and hunger should soon disappear in the world. All wealth which is now used to buy weapons each year can be spent on improvement of agriculture and search for finding new energy sources. The wealth can be used to explore space instead of killing each other. I think the international government can be the existing United Nations with absolute and full authority. All nations in the world with different religions and ethnic background can send their elected members to this international agency. All existing titles such as king, president, queens, and religious leaders should be omitted in the nations and a group of elected members of the United Nation should actually govern the world. The existing advanced communities, such as western nations, should help poor nations to build up their communities and improve their agriculture.

I am sure that sociologist and people who are dealing with human behaviors do not agree with my idea and may even consider it a useless thought. They may say that removal of the borders causes movement of the whole world population into the United States. They may be right to some extent, but if the world reaches to a conclusion that a single government should control the world's affair, the same government can find a solution. The major cause of existing problems in the world is the actions of leaders of certain nations who try to purchase modern weapons to hold their power and prestige. These types of leaders are dangerous for humanity. An international government should remove these types of leaders who came to power by force. The international government should have the authority to review the religious, social, and cultural issues around the world and organize the nations. We should not forget that most people in the world are searching for a quiet and peaceful environment for themselves and their children. The main problem which most nations have is their leaders. There is no doubt that a leader who so far directly or indirectly killed over one million people with different types of weapons—including chemical ones- has some sort of mental disorder and international communities should remove such a leader in a matter of days and before unpredicted things take place.

Obviously, the program of a single government cannot be successful in days, months or even years. In practice, several years is needed to establish a united world. I also do not agree with the ideas that most of the world population will try to move to better locations in the world if no border exist between the nations. In contrast, I think many scientists, engineers, and physicians who left their birth places and moved to western countries because of political reasons and lack of freedom, will go back to their home lands to help their nations.

The idea of a world government is not something new and made by the author of this book. The concept of creating a global political agency, which practices the common rules of laws and has the power and ability to order and promote peace in the world, is not something new. This idea was first presented by the Italian writer Dante Alighieri in the 14th century. This idea was later emphasized in the 17th century by English philosopher Thomas Hobbes who thought mankind should follow a single set of laws in order for everyone to live together peaceably. This idea has also been promoted by other people such as Dutch Hugo Grotius (17th century), French philosophers Jean-Jacques Rousseau (18th century) and Immanuel Kant of Germany (20th century). All these people reached such a conclusion after studying the global wars. After World War I in 1918, the United States President Woodrow Wilson presented the idea of the League of Nations to establish the nations' securities and arms reduction. He thought that the relation between nations should not be based on the balance of power. He proposed that nations should act together for common principles. Opponents in the United States did not agree with Wilson's idea and therefore his idea failed to acquire the effective strength. At the end of World War II (1945), with the formation of the United Nations (UN), the idea of world government got new support. It worth it to mention that many famous people such as Albert Einstein, Bertrand Russell, and Robert Maynard Hutchins had the world government ideas and in practice helped to organize a one-world organization. In general, they argued that there should be an international control of military force, especially nuclear weapons, and the disputes between nations should be resolved peacefully.

Critics dismissed their ideas and considered their thoughts as an impractical dream and impossible. They said such a government would destroy the cultural values and freedom of the nations. Many

Americans opposed such an idea because of its problems associated with trade, and finance. Despite all oppositions, the United Nations was created in 1945. Since its establishment, the United Nations gained some central role in world affairs and tried to unite the world. Its main mission is maintenance of world peace, promotion of good relations between nations, and encourages respect for human rights. Although this organization was established for an overall better life for all human beings, and many of its bodies actually did extensive work for humans all around the world, it has not been a successful organization and what it was meant to be. In 1998 the United Nations had 185 members.

According to the United Nations rules, each member has an equal voice and vote. Unfortunately, this organization could not settle the disputes peacefully in many areas around the world. Although each member of the United Nations is expected to follow the United Nations' decisions and support it, we have seen on many occasions that certain countries did not follow the United Nations orders. I think United Nations should receive full power or authority by its members to remove the leaders of the nations (states) who do not follow the international laws. I think the first action of a powerful United Nations should be inspection of private and government weapons of any kind and their disposal. Only a small international army, which works under the control of the United Nations, is enough for the world. This army should be powerful enough to destroy any wrong doing in a matter of days in any part of the world. The same powerful international government should be able to transfer the technology to different parts of the world and improve the way people live. I am sure if only a fraction of what is used in the wars is spent on research, mankind will soon find a cheap and easily available source of energy. In this case, the crude oil will only be used for petrochemical products. Educated people know that one of the major reasons for many wars in recent years is oil. Both providers and buyers have issues related to oil. Interestingly, the oil reserves will be finished soon. If humans continue what they are doing now, who knows what will be the consequence of their actions, maybe the destruction of the species. I think the actions of humans in the last century created lots of new physical and environmental problems. One may ask, whether human beings' behaviors will finally destroy the global civilization that they themselves have created or not. I hope humans see the constant peace on earth and expand their discoveries in space to solve a portion of mysteries about the existence of the universe which we are a tiny part of.

ABOUT THE AUTHOR

Mehdi Alem is a distinguished microbiologist. His undergraduate studies have been in the field of Biology (BS in General Biology and MS in Radiobiology). He has received a Ph.D. degree in Microbiology from the University of Kent, United Kingdom and has had Postdoctoral trainings in Medical Microbiology at Colorado State University, USA and University of Reading, UK.

Throughout his career, Dr. Alem has been a scientist, director, and associate professor at various universities, clinical laboratories, and medical diagnostic enterprises. He has been the author and co-author of many articles and books on a wide range of topics related to Biology, Medicine and Medical Microbiology.

Dr. Alem is currently the President and CEO of a medical diagnostic company located in the Southern California.

Other books by Mehdi Alem:

1. Wormhole Pass
2. Xbola
3. Met My Father at Age 46
4. Life Inside our Bodies
5. Alien Son-In-Law